PROCEDURES

Lawrence G. Wrenn

Canon Law Society of America
Washington, D.C. 20064

In ore duorum vel trium testium stet omne verbum

Mt. 18, 16

CONTENTS

Preface

PREFACE

The Church's total procedural law deals with contentious cases properly so called, penal cases, cases involving the nullity of ordination and the removal and transfer of pastors, and with various types of marriage cases.

This little volume does not attempt to deal with all of that. Rather it confines itself (except for two appendices on the Petrine Privilege, which were included for convenience's sake) to formal marriage nullity trials. It is hoped that by limiting the field, a clearer picture will emerge.

Even with the field so limited, however, this handbook does not pretend to discuss exhaustively all of the various offices and proceedings involved in such trials. It is, rather, a selective treatment of what appear to be the more important and practical aspects of a marriage case. It is, in short, a primer on who does what and how.

Procedures is written in the style of *Annulments* in that each chapter begins with "The Pertinent Canons". This is meant to highlight the overriding importance of the canons themselves. Always the canons should be read first; the commentary assumes a knowledge of them.

A handbook like this will perhaps be most useful to young canonists or paraprofessionals who have not had a great deal of experience in tribunal work, but I hope that the compactness of the volume, the topical treatment and the ease of locating a given subject by a quick check of the Table of Contents will make it a helpful volume for more experienced personnel as well.

In the commentary I have attempted, not always successfully, I'm sure, to be reasonably practical without being so specific as to endorse one approach rather than another, and to be reasonably objective without altogether abandoning personal opinion.

I wish to thank The Canon Law Society of America for allowing me to use some of my observations which had appeared originally in the CLSA Commentary. I would also like to call attention to the fact that the articles appearing on pages 86 and 114 first appeared in *The Jurist.*

Lawrence G. Wrenn

Hartford, Connecticut
March 4, 1987
Ash Wednesday

INTRODUCTION

AN HISTORICAL OVERVIEW OF COURT PROCEDURES
IN MARRIAGE CASES

The history of the involvement of Church tribunals in marriage cases is an interesting one and may be viewed under the following seven historical stages or eras:

1. **The Early Centuries** (1st - 3rd) — PASTORAL
   a. In the early centuries of Christianity, Church courts dealt basically with two types of cases. The *first* type, called a "contentious" case, involved a controversy between two individual Christians. According to St. Matthew's Gospel, Jesus himself laid down the basic procedural rules to be followed in such cases:

   > *If your brother should commit some wrong against you, go and point out his fault, but keep it between the two of you. If he listens to you, you have won your brother over. If he does not listen, summon another, so that every case may stand on the word of two or three witnesses. If he ignores them, refer it to the church. If he ignores even the church, then treat him as you would a Gentile or a tax collector. I assure you, whatever you declare bound on earth shall be held bound in heaven, and whatever you declare loosed on earth shall be held loosed in heaven.*[1]

   During the early centuries of Christianity these words of Jesus became the guiding principle of Church courts in dealing with all contentious cases.

   The *second* type of case handled by Church courts was the disciplinary case, i.e., the case in which a crime was committed, a crime that distressed the community; and the community then felt some legal action was in order. An example of this type of case is found in I Corinthians 5 where Paul tells the Christians in Corinth that they should sit in judgment of the incestuous man and expel him from their midst.

   b. The process used in both contentious and disciplinary cases was basically the same. There would be an initial attempt at conciliation and, if that proved unsuccessful, the case would then go to court. Often there was a collegiate tribunal consisting of a bishop, a priest and a deacon. The Gospel directive about the two or three witnesses was always observed but in places like Greece, Egypt and Syria local judicial traditions were followed as well.

   c. Some cases heard in Church courts dealt with marital matters, like the incestuous man at Corinth, but there were no marriage cases as such, i.e., cases dealing with the question of possible invalidity. Church courts *were* in place and could be utilized to judge marriage nullity cases if and when they arose but it's important to note that the procedures followed in Church courts at that time were designed not for marriage cases but for contentious and disciplinary cases.

1

2. **The Age of Constantine** (4th and 5th) — ROMAN

   a. After Constantine converted, and Christianity became an approved religion with close ties to the Empire, Church courts tended to adopt more and more of the procedures found in Roman law, like for example, the petition, the citation and the appeal. Nevertheless certain local customs were still retained in various Christian centers.

   b. Disciplinary cases, especially those involving heretics, were, by far, the most prevalent. The notion of marriage as being indissoluble was still not fully developed and marriage cases as we know them were still non-existent.

3. **The Middle Ages** (6th - 11th) — MUDDLED

   a. With the fall of the Roman Empire, the invasion of Europe by the tribes from the north and their eventual conversion to Christianity, new legal traditions were introduced into the Church, especially the Germanic traditions of trial by ordeal and trial by compurgation. Today we tend to see these Germanic traditions as primitive, and as grossly inferior to Roman law, in that Roman law attached great importance to the judge and to the judge's reasonable decisions whereas Germanic law tended to diminish the role of the judge, attaching prevailing importance instead either to magic, chance or God (in the case of ordeal) or (in the case of compurgation) to the number of people who would swear in behalf of the parties.

   But the differences between Roman law and Germanic law were, in fact, much more profound and pervasive than that. On this point Harold J. Berman writes:

   > Law was for the peoples of Europe, in the early stages of their history, not primarily a matter of making and applying rules in order to determine guilt and fix judgment, not an instrument to separate people from one another on the basis of a set of principles, but rather a matter of holding people together, a matter of reconciliation. Law was conceived primarily as a mediating process, a mode of communication, rather than primarily as a process of rule-making and decision-making.

   In these respects, Germanic and other European folklaw had much in common with certain Eastern legal philosophies. In the Sufi tradition of the Middle East, one of the stories told of the Mulla Nasrudin depicts him as a magistrate hearing his first case. The plaintiff argues so persuasively that Nasrudin exclaims, "I believe you are right." The clerk of the court begs him to restrain himself, since the defendant is yet to be heard. Listening to the defendant's argument, Nasrudin is again so carried away that he cries out, "I believe you are right." The clerk of the court cannot allow this. "Your honor," he says, "they cannot both be right." "I believe you are right," Nasrudin replies.

2

Both are right, yet both cannot be right. The answer is not to be found by asking the question, Who is right? The answer is to be found by saving the honor of both sides and thereby restoring the right relationship between them.[2]

In much the same way Germanic folklaw was interested not so much in determining objective rights or facts as it was in bringing harmony into individual and social relationships. It was a system vastly different from Roman law, and yet during the Middle Ages both systems were used sort of side by side, in an uneasy, awkward arrangement.

b. It also bears noting that during the course of these same centuries (to complicate the matter even further) the texts of Roman law were lost, and lawyers came then to have only a fragmented knowledge of the Roman legal system. This, of course, muddled the procedural picture even further.

c. During the Middle Ages, therefore, court procedures were influenced by a wide array of legal traditions — Roman, canonical, local and Germanic, many of which were poorly understood. And, as a result, the procedures that were actually followed in individual cases were, to a great extent, left to the discretion of the judge.

d. Perhaps there were some marriage cases heard in Church courts during this period but if so they were quite isolated and would have involved only members of the noble class. Certainly cases were brought before Church councils regarding such matters as degrees of invalidating consanguinity and affinity, and whether consummation was required for validity but marriage cases brought before local tribunals were, at best, few and far between, and little is known of court procedures as applied to marriage cases during this period.[3]

e. The main point is this: that in the days prior to Gratian's Decree there were many, often conflicting legal traditions influencing the courts and consequently a great deal of confusion. As a result, a "praxis paterna" developed leaving judges considerable freedom in investigating and adjudicating cases.[4]

4. **The Early Classical Age** (12th - 13th) — RIGID

a. When, during this period, the Roman law texts themselves were "rediscovered," and interpretation of them was raised to an art, and when, coincidentally, the Church's influence was solidified under Gregory VII, Roman law became, hands down, the *major* source for Church law and specifically for the procedural law to be followed in Church courts. A great scholarship developed in this field and, for a century or so, a period of extreme rigidity set in. Courts did a complete flip-flop. Whereas in the *tenth* century courts followed a "praxis paterna," by the *thirteenth* century, courts were following a strict "praxis canonica" which was in effect, an ecclesiastical adaptation of classical Roman law.

3

b. By this time, furthermore, marriage had come to be recognized first of all as indissoluble and secondly as one of the seven sacraments. During this period, therefore, it came to be widely accepted that marriage cases fell under the jurisdiction not of the civil courts but of the church courts, and there is considerable evidence during this period that marriage cases as we know them, were now being heard in the tribunals of the Church.

c. The main point is this: that during this Early Classical Age two things happened: 1) for the first time in the Church's history, cases of marriage nullity came to be heard in significant numbers and 2) the procedures followed in the courts in adjudicating those cases were highly technical and very rigid. This is the situation that prevailed throughout most of the thirteenth century.

5. **The Later Classical Age** (14th - 15th) — INFORMAL

a. Very early on in the fourteenth century there was a reaction on the part of Rome to this procedural rigidity. By way of background it is useful to remember that, following the great centralization of power under such popes as Gregory VII and Innocent III, local tribunals were competent to hear only minor cases. All major cases were reserved to the Pope. In practice, however, the Pope often delegated many of these cases back to the local tribunals. The *Corpus Iuris Canonici* contains a decretal of Pope Boniface VIII (who died in 1303) in which he instructed a local court to hear a case "sine strepitu iudicii et figura" or, as we might say, "without the pomp and circumstance of a judicial proceeding."[5] This directive of Boniface VIII is the first known instance of a Pope saying, in effect, that the strict procedural law that had developed during the previous century or so might be dispensed with in a particular case.

b. Over the next few years it appears that several such dispensations were granted and in all cases the phrase "sine strepitu iudicii et figura" was used. There was, however, widespread confusion over what exactly that phrase meant so, in 1306, Pope Clement V issued the famous decretal *Saepe Contingit* in which he spelled out the precise meaning of the phrase. The decretal reads as follows:

> It often happens that we delegate lower courts to hear cases, and in some of those cases we order those courts to proceed simply and easily and without the pomp and circumstance of a judicial proceeding. The precise meaning of these words, however, is a matter of considerable debate and there is some question therefore about how courts ought to proceed.

> In the interest of settling as many of those questions as possible, we, by this decree, hereby declare as sacred and perpetual that a judge to whom we commit cases of this kind: need not necessarily demand a formal libellus or a joinder of issues; may proceed even on holidays in order to accommodate the needs of people who have been dispensed by the law; may shorten deadlines; may, to the extent that he can, shorten the trial by denying exceptions and

4

dilatory and unnecessary appeals, and by restricting the contentions and disputes of the parties, advocates and procurators, and by limiting the number of witnesses.

A judge may not, however, abbreviate a trial by curtailing necessary proofs or legitimate defenses. Lest the truth remain concealed, furthermore, it is understood, that in commissions of this kind neither the citation nor the taking of the usual oaths of good faith and intent, and to tell the truth may ever be omitted. Also, since the pronouncement of the judge ought to be based on the original petition, the plaintiff's position, and that of the respondent if he or she countersues, should be made at the beginning of the trial either in writing or orally and should always be included in the acts. This is important for three reasons: so that the investigation may be based on those petitions, so that fuller certitude may be had, and so that the issue may be more clearly defined. And because traditional judicial practice has allowed the use of questionnaires, based on the statements of the parties, for the purpose of expediting the proceedings, as well as interrogatories for the purpose of obtaining clearer proofs, we, wishing to follow this practice, hereby declare that any judge deputed by us (unless he proceeds otherwise at the wish of the parties) may establish a deadline for submitting these questionnaires and interrogatories as well as for all other acts and defenses which the parties wish to be used in the case. After these articles have been submitted the judge may then assign an appropriate date for producing witnesses, with the understanding, however, that should the case be interrupted, those witnesses, and documents as well, may be produced at a later date. The judge shall also question the parties either at their request or ex officio whenever equity recommends this.

Finally the judge, either standing or sitting, as he pleases, will hand down the written definitive sentence (with both parties having been cited for this action though not peremptorily) based on the petition, the proofs and other pleadings in the case. This he shall do even if, in his judgment, the evidence is not concluded.

All of which is also applicable to all those cases in which, through one or another of our constitutions, it is allowed that a judge may proceed simply and easily and without the pomp and circumstance of a judicial proceeding. But if, in these cases, the solemn judicial order is, in fact, observed, in whole or in part, with the parties not disagreeing, the process will not, on that account, be either void or voidable.[6]

c. Within another five years it had become apparent that this less formal procedure (which came to be called the Clementine procedure) was working quite well. Pope Clement therefore decided that, rather than give dispensations for its use on an ad hoc basis, he would grant a general permission for all courts to use this informal procedure in certain types of cases (which, in fact, included most cases). Clement did this in 1311 in his decretal *Dispendiosam,* which reads as follows:

In the interest of reducing the lengthy delays in court trials which sometimes result, as evidence has shown, from a scrupulous application of the judicial process to individual cases, we hereby decree that, regarding not only future cases but present cases as well and even those cases pending appeal, a court may proceed simply and easily and without the pomp and circumstance of a judicial proceeding in the following cases: those regarding elections, postulations, provisions, dignities, personates, offices, canonicates, revenues or any ecclesiastical benefices, the exacting of tithes (including the possibility, after a proper warning, of coercing payment by ecclesiastical censure from those who are in arrears) and finally marriage and usury cases and all those touching on them in any way.[7]

d. From the year 1311 on, then, practically all marriage cases were heard not by the formal process but by the Clementine or informal process. Indeed, at some times and in some places even the Clementine process was not followed but something less formal and judicial than that.

6. The Tridentine and Post Tridentine Age (16th - 19th) — CENTRALIZED

a. By the time of the Council of Trent (1563) marriage cases were, in some places, being heard by deans and archdeacons, sometimes without following a judicial process. The Council of Trent ordered that, in the future, all marriage cases would be heard only at the diocesan level, and, in all cases, the judicial procedure (not necessarily the formal but at least the informal or Clementine judicial procedure) should be followed.[8]

b. Abuses, however, persisted and, in an effort to curb them, Pope Benedict XIV issued, on November 3, 1741, his famous constitution *Dei miseratione*.[9] Benedict was particularly upset by the facility with which annulments were being granted in his day. Oftentimes the respondent would not appear at the trial at all, so there would be no one to defend the marriage (there was, in those days, no one designated as a defender of the bond). Sometimes both parties would appear, but either the respondent would be in collusion with the petitioner, or he or she would simply not be interested in appealing higher and the marriage would then be declared null after a single hearing (there was, in those days, no mandatory appeal). As a result, according to Benedict, men and women alike were having their first, second, and even third marriages declared null and were, with the blessing of the Church, blithely entering still another.

Dei miseratione attempted to put an end to all this. First it required that every diocese appoint a defender of marriage whose presence in every trial would be absolutely mandatory and whose duty it would be to defend the bond. Secondly, it required the defender to appeal every first instance affirmative decision.

It bears noting, however, that marriage cases were heard in those days not by three judges but by one. This, indeed, would remain the law of the Church until the 1917 code.

It further bears noting that the scandalous situation that existed prior to *Dei miseratione* seems to have been due at least partly to the fact that there was, at the time, no process in Church courts that was specifically designed for the hearing of marriage cases. One of Benedict's principal contributions, therefore, was that, in introducing the office of defensor matrimonii and the notion of mandatory appeal, he was, for the first time, adding to the procedural law of the Church elements that referred specifically to marriage cases. Predictably it resulted in a significant improvement in the system.

c. In 1840 the Congregation of the Council issued a new Instruction, *Cum moneat,*[10] designed to reinforce, clarify and amplify *Dei miseratione.* The United States, however, was still mission territory and in this country, therefore, marriage cases were, at least until 1884, still being settled in the rectory with no judicial formalities whatsoever.

d. In 1884 the Congregation for the Propagation of the Faith issued for this country the Instruction *Causae Matrimoniales*[11] which, in effect, required that all marriage cases be heard by the diocesan tribunal using the Clementine process along with the adjustments required by *Dei miseratione* (i.e., the presence of a defender and a mandatory appeal of an affirmative decision). *Causae Matrimoniales* was the last significant document pertinent to marriage trials prior to the codification in 1917 of the Church's law.

7. **The Age of the Codes** (20th) — RIGID

a. By the turn of the century the ordinary process had lapsed altogether into desuetude, and only the summary process was being used, in marriage cases and almost all other types of cases as well.

b. In their pre-Code manuals, Lega and Wernz both devoted brief sections to the special procedures followed in marriage cases. Lega was satisfied with simply reprinting *Causae Matrimoniales,* noting that it was practically the same as previous instructions issued for the Oriental Churches and for Austria. Wernz, on the other hand, wrote his own treatment on the procedures to be followed in marriage cases, in which he commented on such matters as the right to petition for an annulment, the competent judge (marriage cases, remember, were heard by a *single* judge) suitable proofs, the involvement of the defender and the mandatory appeal of an affirmative decision.

c. The 1917 Code made a kind of amalgam of the summary process and the old ordinary process, thereby making the process more formal than it had been in centuries. Among other things, it required, in C. 1576 §1, that all marriage nullity cases be heard by a college of three judges "with every contrary custom being reprobated and every contrary privilege revoked." But, like the pre-Code authors, it also devoted a separate section, namely, canons 1960-1992, to marriage trials in particular, in which it treated briefly the predictable issues of competence, court personnel, the right to petition, proofs, publication, the conclusion in causa, the sentence, the appeal, and, finally, certain clear cases, like prior bond, that could be proved by document and could therefore be handled informally.

d. By 1936 the Holy See, realizing that around the world very few marriage cases were being handled judicially by local tribunals, concluded that the thirty-three canons of the 1917 Code (canons 1960-1992) devoted specifically to marriage cases, were not sufficient to aid the local judge in applying the canons on trials in general (canons 1552-1924) to marriage cases. Accordingly, on August 15, 1936, the Holy See issued a new Instruction, *Provida mater*[12], which consisted of two hundred forty articles that attempted, in effect, to rewrite general procedure as it might apply to marriage cases. *Provida mater* was a valiant and, no doubt, well-intentioned effort to assist local judges, but the rigidity and complexity of the Instruction seemed to discourage judges even more, and thousands of bona fide marriage cases continued to go unheard. In the United States, for example, where, by the late 1960s, there were an estimated five million divorced Catholics, only a few hundred first instance affirmative decisions were being given each year.

e. In an effort to correct this situation, the Canon Law Society of America endorsed, at its annual meeting in 1968, a simple set of norms, called the *American Procedural Norms*, with the request that the National Conference of Catholic Bishops propose them to Rome for approval. Approval was given, effective July 1, 1970, first for a three-year experimental period, then in 1973 for one more year, and finally in 1974, until the new procedural law for the Church universal would be promulgated. The aim of the *American Procedural Norms* was, on the one hand, to provide adequate defense of the marriage bond and thus avoid the scandalous sort of annulment that existed before *Dei miseratione*, but, on the other hand, to provide to tribunals a procedure that could be carried out "simpliciter et de plano, ac sine strepitu iudicii et figura," and could thus enable them to give a hearing to the many thousands of people with legitimate grounds of annulment. The principal features of the *American Procedural Norms* were the recognition of the petitioner's residence as a source of competence, trial by a single judge, discretionary appeal by the defender. The *American Procedural Norms* were dramatically successful. By the late 1970s, thirty thousand annulments a year were being granted, judicially and judiciously, by United States tribunals. Although that figure was still only one-half of one percent of the number of divorced Catholics in the country (six million by that time), the *American Procedural Norms* were, nevertheless, of benefit to a great many people.

f. Americans were not the only ones interested in simplified procedures. There was considerable interest around the world in providing for a more expeditious handling of marriage cases, and on March 28, 1971, Pope Paul VI issued, for the universal Church, the Apostolic Letter *Causas matrimoniales* which was not as liberal in its provisions as the *American Procedural Norms*, but which did modify the prescriptions of the 1917 Code in the areas of competence, the number of judges, the use of lay people, and the appellate procedures.

By this time, of course, the work of revising the 1917 Code, specifically its procedural law, was well under way and when the 1976 schema on procedural law appeared, it contained, as was expected, the modifications introduced by *Causas matrimoniales*. Most of these have, in turn, been incorporated into the 1983 Code.

g. The 1983 Code, however, still requires that marriage cases be processed in accord with procedural rules that were designed for contentious cases. This unfortunate and apparently artificial arrangement, which seems to favor the system over the needs of people, prevents, in the opinion of this author, Book VII of the 1983 Code (unlike the Code as a whole) from moving on to Stage Eight which would be characterized as PASTORAL.

ENDNOTES

1. Mt. 18: 15-18.

2. Harold J. Berman, *Law and Revolution* (Cambridge, Harvard University Press, 1983), p. 78.

3. George H. Joyce, *Christian Marriage* (London, Sheed and Ward, 1933) pp. 214-236.

4. Charles Lefebvre "De Iudicio Reddendo in Ecclesia (Lineamenta Historica)," *Monitor Ecclesiasticus* 1972, II-III, p. 228.

5. VI°, 1, 6, 43.

6. Clem. V, 11, 2.

7. Clem. II, 1, 2.

8. Session XXIV, ch. 20.

9. Fontes I, n. 318, 695-701.

10. Fontes VI, n. 4069, 345-350.

11. Fontes VII, n. 4901, 479-492.

12. CLD 2, 471-529.

COMPETENCE

A. The Pertinent Canon

C.1673 — In cases regarding the nullity of marriage which are not reserved to the Apostolic See the following are competent:

1° the tribunal of the place in which the marriage was celebrated;
2° the tribunal of the place in which the respondent has a domicile or quasi-domicile;
3° the tribunal of the place in which the petitioner has a domicile, provided that both parties live in the territory of the same conference of bishops and the judicial vicar of the domicile of the respondent agrees, after hearing the respondent;
4° the tribunal of the place in which de facto most of the proofs are to be collected provided that the judicial vicar of the domicile of the respondent gives consent who, before he does so, is to ask if the respondent has any exceptions.

B. Definition

Competence may be defined as the portion of jurisdiction assigned to each tribunal. Competence, therefore, designates the extent or limits of activity permitted each tribunal.

C. Sources Of Competence

The law is the source — it gives 4 ways

According to C. 1673, there are, in a marriage case, four sources of competence: the place of *marriage,* the domicile or quasi-domicile of the *respondent,* the domicile of the *petitioner,* and the place of *proofs.*

This does not mean, of course, that, in every marriage case, there are always four different tribunals involved. Oftentimes, indeed, all four sources of competence are within the *same* diocese. When, however, more than one tribunal is competent, then the petitioner is free to choose. Petitioners generally choose to introduce a case in their *own* tribunal (of domicile — 3°) but occasionally, perhaps because their own tribunal has a large backlog and is processing cases slowly, a petitioner might elect to lodge his or her petition elsewhere.

Although the four sources of competence are not listed in any strict hierarchical order, still it should be noted that the first two (marriage and respondent) are absolute sources while the latter two (petitioner and proofs) are conditioned sources, that is to say, that certain provisos are attached to their use.

1. The Tribunal of Marriage

A petition may always be lodged in the tribunal of the diocese within whose territory the marriage in question took place. The specific place of marriage need not, of course, always be a Catholic church ((two Protestants, for example, might have married before a minister or a justice of the peace), but, in a convalidation, the place of marriage that qualifies the tribunal as competent is the place not of the first ceremony but of the convalidation ceremony. A Catholic couple, for example, might go through a civil ceremony in San Francisco and have the marriage validated in Chicago. The competent tribunal by reason of place of marriage would be not San Francisco but Chicago.

2. The Tribunal of the Respondent

Competence arises either from the domicile or even from the quasi-domicile (C. 102) of the respondent. If, in fact, the respondent has multiple fora, the petitioner may choose any one of them (C. 1407 § 3). For this source of competence to be operative, however, the residence of the respondent must be in effect at the time of the citation. See "The Effects of the Citation" on page 39.

3. The Tribunal of the Petitioner

Several points are to be noted here:

a. It is only the domicile, not the quasi-domicile of the petitioner that establishes a title to competence.

b. An essential condition in order for this title to become operative is the requirement that the other party reside in the same episcopal conference. If, therefore, the specific whereabouts of the respondent are unknown but there is no reason to suspect that he or she resides outside the territory of the U.S. Conference then this condition may be regarded as fulfilled. If, however, there is some indication that the respondent resides outside that territory, then this source of competence may not be utilized.

c. Puerto Rico, though part of the United States, has its own episcopal conference (Conferencia Episcopal Puertorriqueña — CEP). In 1984 the NCCB and the CEP jointly requested from the Signatura an indult which would enable a marriage case involving a petitioner and a respondent in which one is domiciled on the mainland and the other in Puerto Rico to be heard in either locality, but the indult was not granted.

d. When the petitioner's domicile is the source of the tribunal's competence the canon requires that the respondent be heard and that the respondent's judicial vicar give consent. These requirements are usually fulfilled by writing a letter to the respondent, a copy of which is sent to the respondent's judicial vicar, explaining that a petition has been received and

11

asking whether the respondent has any objection to the case being heard in the petitioner's tribunal. The respondent is supplied with the address of his or her own tribunal and is advised, if he or she *does* object, to contact that tribunal within, say, two weeks. The respondent is also advised that if the petitioner's tribunal does not hear from the respondent's tribunal in, say, three weeks, the consent of the respondent's judicial vicar will be presumed.

A sample of this letter may be found as Document One on page 126.

    e. As with the respondent, in order for this source of competence to be valid, the petitioner must be domiciled in the diocese at the time of the citation.

4. *The Tribunal of Proofs*

    a. The phrase "the place in which de facto most of the proofs are to be collected" is a broad one which ought not to be abused. It would, for example, be illicit for a tribunal which would otherwise have no jurisdiction whatever over a case, to request pre-trial affidavits from all potential witnesses, and then claim, since it was in possession of those affidavits at the time the respondent was cited (at which moment the trial officially opens — C. 1512) that it thereby enjoyed competence by reason of C.1673, 4°.

On the other hand, should a tribunal in good faith request those same affidavits in behalf of a petitioner domiciled in its diocese, that tribunal could legitimately claim competence by reason of C. 1673, 4° if the petitioner moved out of the diocese prior to the citation of the respondent.

    b. Generally speaking, however, this source is used only when at least two of the witnesses or affiants actually reside in the diocese.

    c. Unlike the tribunal of the petitioner, the tribunal of proofs may be utilized even if the respondent does not reside within the territory of the same episcopal conference.

    d. As regards contacting the respondent and his or her judicial vicar, C. 1673, 4° indicates that, in this case, respondents should be contacted not by the judicial vicar of the tribunal of proofs but by their *own* judicial vicar. The approach of the tribunal of proofs is therefore somewhat different from that of the tribunal of the petitioner (see above - section C3d). In this case the letter is written not to the respondent but to the respondent's judicial vicar explaining the matter and requesting the judicial vicar to contact the respondent.

For a sample of such a letter see Document Two on page 127.

JUDICIAL VICAR

A. The Pertinent Canons

C. 1420 — §1. Each diocesan bishop is bound to appoint a judicial vicar or officialis with ordinary power to judge, distinct from the vicar general unless the smallness of the diocese or the small number of cases suggests otherwise.

§2. The judicial vicar constitutes one tribunal with the bishop but he cannot judge cases which the bishop reserves to himself.

§3. The judicial vicar can be given assistants whose title is adjutant judicial vicars or vice-officiales.

§4. Both the judicial vicar and the adjutant judicial vicars must be priests of unimpaired reputations, holding doctorates or at least licentiates in canon law and not less than thirty years of age.

§5. When the see is vacant, they do not cease from their office and they cannot be removed by the diocesan administrator; when the new bishop arrives, however, they need confirmation.

C. 1422 — The judicial vicar, the adjutant judicial vicars and the other judges are to be appointed for a definite period of time with due regard for the prescription of C. 1420, §5; they cannot be removed except for legitimate and serious cause.

B. Definition

The diocesan judicial vicar, otherwise known as the officialis, is a priest appointed by the diocesan bishop to judge cases with ordinary power and to serve (in conjunction with the bishop) as the chief judge of the diocese.

C. Qualities

The judicial vicar, as is clear from C. 1420 §4, must be a) a priest b) of unimpaired reputation, c) having at least a JCL and d) not less than 30 years of age.

D. Term Of Office

C. 1422 notes that a judicial vicar should be appointed for a definite term of office.

It has, unfortunately, become a not uncommon practice in the United States for an officialis to serve in that capacity for only a limited number of years (one or two brief terms) and then to move on to parish work or some other apostolate, partly, perhaps, because tribunal work is not the most rewarding of ministries. This, however, creates a problem: since learning the law and building judicial skills is the work of a lifetime (requiring both scholarship and the putting of that scholarship into practice in a sensitive way) this kind of mobility, not only among officiales but among other court officers as well, often results in a serious lack of professionalism in American tribunals. By way of correcting this problem, it is to be hoped that more people will, in the future, devote a significant portion of their lives to this healing, truly pastoral work.

E. Scope

Traditionally, the work of the officialis has been seen as both judicial and administrative (see, for example, Goyeneche, *De Processibus,* 1, p. 70). The officialis has, in other words, been both the chief judge and the chief administrator of the tribunal's activities.

In recent years, however, some tribunals have introduced the seemingly legitimate practice of separating the two functions, with one person (meeting all the qualifications of C. 1420 §4) serving as chief *judicial* officer, and another person (possessing administrative skills and often a lay person) serving as chief *executive* officer.

There are, no doubt, both advantages and disadvantages to this system; its prudent use would depend on circumstances.

JUDGE

A. The Pertinent Canons

C. 1421 — §1. The bishop is to appoint diocesan judges in the diocese who are clerics.

§2. The conference of bishops can permit lay persons to be appointed judges; when it is necessary, one of them can be employed to form a collegiate tribunal.

§3. The judges are to be of unimpaired reputation and possess doctorates, or at least licentiates, in canon law.

C. 1422 — The judicial vicar, the adjutant judicial vicars and the other judges are to be appointed for a definite period of time with due regard for the prescription of C. 1420 §5; they cannot be removed except for legitimate and serious cause.

C. 1424 — In any trial a single judge can make use of two assessors, who are clerics or lay persons of upright life, to serve as his consultors.

C. 1425 — §1. Every contrary custom being reprobated, the following cases are reserved to a collegiate tribunal of three judges:

1° contentious cases: a) concerning the bond of sacred ordination; b) concerning the bond of marriage with due regard for the prescriptions of canons 1686 and 1688;

2° penal cases: a) concerning offenses which can entail the penalty of dismissal from the clerical state; b) concerning the imposition or declaration of excommunication.

§3. Unless the bishop has determined otherwise for individual cases, the judicial vicar is to assign the judges in order by turn to adjudicate the individual cases.

§4. If it happens that a collegiate tribunal cannot be established for a trial of first instance, the conference of bishops can permit the bishop to entrust cases to a single clerical judge as long as the impossibility of establishing a college perdures; he is to be a cleric and is to employ an assessor and an auditor where possible.

§5. The judicial vicar is not to appoint substitutes for judges once they are assigned unless for a most serious reason, expressed in a decree.

C. 1426 — §1. A collegiate tribunal must proceed as a collegial body and pass its sentences by majority vote.

§2. The judicial vicar or the adjutant judicial vicar must preside over a collegiate tribunal insofar as this is possible.

B. Definition

An ecclesiastical judge is a person appointed by the diocesan bishop to hear and decide cases brought to the ecclesiastical court.

C. Qualities

There is no minimum age requirement for the office of judge. Neither is it required that a judge be a member of the clergy. A layperson may serve as judge. It is, however, required that a judge a) be of unimpaired reputation and b) have at least a JCL.

D. The Lay Person As Judge

The canons indicate that, per se, a judge should be a cleric. Per accidens, however, that is to say, when necessity requires it, a lay person may be appointed as judge.

The lay judge, it should be noted, may not serve as a single judge (C. 1425, §4) but only as one of three judges on a college, with the other two judges on that college being clerics (C. 1421 §§1 and 2).

This legislation has given rise to two different opinions regarding the role of the lay judge.

The first opinion states that when a lay person is appointed a judge, she or he is cooperating in the power of governance (jurisdiction) in accord with C. 129 §2 but in a peculiar way, namely in a way that contradicts C. 274 §1 which states that only clerics can obtain offices for whose exercise jurisdiction is required. In the case of C. 1421 §2, says this opinion, we clearly have a lay person being given an inherently jurisdictional office (James H. Provost, "The Participation of the Laity in the Governance of the Church," *Studia Canonica,* 1983, 437-438).

Furthermore, says this first opinion, the Code nowhere restricts the activity of the lay judge beyond requiring that a lay judge serve always as one judge on a college, never as a single judge. The Code does not, for example, say that a lay judge may not serve as the *presiding* judge of the college. In accord, therefore, with the axiom "Iure permittuntur quae iure non prohibentur," the lay judge may serve as presiding judge and may, therefore, designate an auditor (C. 1428), deal with an objection against a judge (C. 1449), accept or reject a libellus (C. 1505), cite the respondent (C. 1507), join the issue (C. 1513 and 1677) and call for and preside over the sentence session (C. 1609).

According to the second opinion the lay judge can do none of these things because, *as an individual,* the lay judge is not empowered to exercise jurisdiction (which is

16

why the law does not permit the lay person to serve as a single judge). The lay judge can serve only on a college and in that case it is not the individuals on the college but rather the (predominantly clerical) college itself which exercises the jurisdiction. There is, therefore, no contradiction between C. 1421 §2 (which allows a lay person to be a judge) and C. 129 §2 (which does not permit a lay person to hold an inherently jurisdictional office) because, although the college exercises jurisdiction, the individual members of the college do not. (David-Maria A. Jaeger, OFM, "Lay People and the Power of Governance: Another View," *(CLSGB&I Newsletter* n. 62, September 1984, p. 31).

These two opinions are, of course, rooted in the much larger dispute regarding the nature of sacred power in the Church and whether or not the power of order and the power of governance are distinct.

E. Duties

The work of the judge is to hear and decide cases by engaging in jurisprudence, i.e., the science and art of utilizing, interpreting and supplying for the codified law by judicial sentence. For more on jurisprudence see *Annulments,* pp. 1-7.

F. Term Of Office

C. 1422 notes that judges are to be appointed for a definite term of office. Under the 1917 Code (C. 1574 §2) the usual term of office for the judge was ten years. That time period might still be regarded as a suitable rule of thumb and would, of course, be renewable.

C. 1420 §5 notes that, when the see is vacant, judges do not lose their office but, when the new bishop arrives, they need confirmation.

INSTRUCTOR

A. The Pertinent Canon

C. 1428 — §1. A judge or the president of a collegiate tribunal can designate an auditor to carry out the instruction of a case, selecting one either from among the judges of the tribunal or from among the persons approved for this function by the bishop.

§2. The bishop can approve for the function of auditor clerics or lay persons who are outstanding for their good character, prudence and learning.

§3. The only task of the auditor is to collect the proofs according to the mandate of the judge and to present them to the judge; unless the mandate of the judge states otherwise, the auditor can in the meantime decide which proofs are to be collected and how they are to be collected if such a question perhaps arises while the auditor is exercising his or her function.

B. Definition

An Instructor or Auditor is a person approved by the bishop and selected by the judge to "instruct" a case, i.e. to gather the proofs and present them to the judge.

C. Usefulness

The question of whether or not it is wise to involve instructors in the judicial process, has long been hotly disputed. Cardinal Roberti, one of the more prestigious of the commentators on the procedural law of the 1917 Code, was of the opinion that judge instructors did more harm than good, since their involvement necessarily resulted in the principal judge losing that immediate contact with the parties and witnesses that is so important in deciding a case. The same argument was made in an attempt to suppress the office of auditor in the 1983 Code at the April 8, 1978 meeting of the consultors of the Commission.

The office has, however, been retained in the 1983 Code, and it has indeed been found immensely useful in some courts for many years now. Some American tribunals employ a great many instructors who are responsible for collecting and presenting all the evidence to the defender of the bond and the judge, thus enabling the court to be of assistance to far more people than would ever be possible if the judge had to do all the auditing personally. Roberti's point is, of course, a valid one but must be weighed against the demands being made on tribunals today to serve such large numbers of petitioners.

D. The Instructor And The Designated Receiver

A Designated Receiver (DR) is a person assigned by the judge to obtain the testimony and affidavit of a person who refused to appear before the judge or instructor (C. 1528).

Clearly the role of the DR is more restricted than that of the instructor, since the DR is only commissioned to obtain evidence from a specific difficult party or witness, whereas the instructor or auditor can not only collect all the proofs available in a given case but even decide, at least in the absence of a specific directive from the judge, which proofs are to be included.

When, incidentally, the instructor is a lay person, this activity of the instructor would seem to be an instance of an individual lay person exercising jurisdiction.

E. The Instructor And The Advocate

The roles of instructor and advocate are obviously quite different. An advocate is appointed by a *party* to protect the rights of and argue the case of that party, whereas the instructor is appointed by the *judge* to collect with judicial impartiality the available evidence. See also page 26.

DEFENDER

A. The Pertinent Canons

C. 1432 — A defender of the bond is to be appointed in a diocese for cases concerning the nullity of sacred ordination or the nullity or dissolution of marriage; the defender of the bond is bound by office to propose and clarify everything which can be reasonably adduced against nullity or dissolution.

C. 1433 — In cases which require the presence of the promoter of justice or the defender of the bond, the acts are invalid if they were not cited, unless, although not cited, they were actually present, or, at least before the sentence, could have fulfilled their office by inspecting the acts.

C. 1434— Unless express provision is made to the contrary:

1° as often as the law requires the judge to hear the parties or one or other of them, the promoter of justice and the defender of the bond are also to be heard if they are present in court;

2° as often as the judge is required to decide something at the request of a party, the request of the promoter of justice or the defender of the bond has the same force when they are present in the court.

C. 1435— It is the task of the bishop to name the promoter of justice and the defender of the bond who are to be clerics or lay persons of unimpaired reputation who hold doctorates or licentiates in canon law and are proven in prudence and in zeal for justice.

C. 1436 — §1. The same person can hold the office of promoter of justice and of defender of the bond but not in the same case.

§2. The promoter and defender can be appointed for all cases or for particular cases; they can, however, be removed by the bishop for a just cause.

C. 1447 — A person who has taken part in a case as a judge, promoter of justice, defender of the bond, procurator, advocate, witness or expert cannot afterwards in another instance validly resolve the same case as a judge or act as an assessor in another instance.

B. Definition

A defender of the bond is a person appointed by the diocesan bishop and assigned by the judicial vicar to a particular case to propose and clarify everything which can be reasonably adduced in favor of the validity of the marriage in question.

C. Qualities

C. 1435 indicates that a defender should a) be a person of unimpaired reputation, b) possess at least a JCL and c) be proven in prudence and in zeal for justice.

D. Principal Duty

The principal duty of the defender is to argue *pro vinculo*. As C. 1432 says, the defender is "bound by office to propose and clarify everything which can be reasonably adduced against nullity."

At the same time, however, the defender should also argue *pro rei veritate,* which is, no doubt, why the canon uses the word "reasonably" — "everything which can be reasonably adduced." Pius XII, in his 1944 allocution, explained it this way:

> It is the competency of the Defender of the Bond to uphold the existence or the continuance of the marriage bond. This, however, is not to be effected in an absolute way but subordinately to the purpose of the process which is the search and the ascertainment of the objective truth.

> The Defender of the Bond must cooperate toward the common end in so far as he investigates, presents and clarifies all that can be adduced in favor of the bond. To enable the Defender of the Bond, who is to be considered as "Pars necessaria ad iudicii validitatem et integritatem," efficaciously to fulfill the duties of his office, procedural law has given him special rights and has assigned to him definite duties. And just as it would not be compatible with the importance of his office and with the vigilant and faithful fulfillment of his duty if he were to be content with a summary scrutiny of the acts and certain superficial observations; so it is likewise not proper that this office be entrusted to those lacking in experience of life and mature judgment. This rule, however, does not do away with the fact that the observations of the Defender of the Bond are to be under the supervision of the Judges, for the Judges must find in the Defender's accurate exposition an aid and a complement to their own work. Nor is it to be expected that the Judges always repeat all the work and all the investigations of the Defender in order that they might be enabled to place trust in his exposition of the case.

> On the other hand, it cannot be demanded of the Defender of the Bond that he draw up a defense at any cost; an artificial defense without care as to whether or not his statements have a solid foundation. Such a demand would be contrary to right reason. It would burden the Defender of the Bond with a useless, worthless task. It would contribute no clarification, but rather a confusion of the question. It would harmfully prolong the process. In the very interest of truth and by the dignity of his office the Defender of the Bond must, therefore, be accorded the right to declare, whenever the case requires, that after a diligent, accurate and conscientious examination of the acts he has

discovered no reasonable objection to be made against the petition of the plaintiff or the petitioner.

This fact and this knowledge of not having unconditionally to defend an imposed thesis, but of being instead at the service of the already existing truth, will spare the Defender of the Bond from proposing questions which would be one-sidedly suggestive and circumventive. It will further spare him from exaggeration and from changing possibilities to probabilities, or even to accomplished facts. This will likewise spare him from asserting or fabricating contradictions in cases where a sound judgment would not discern them or would easily resolve them.

It will spare him from impugning the veracity of the witnesses, because of discrepancies or inaccuracies in points nonessential or unimportant to the object of the process, discrepancies and inaccuracies which are proved by the psychology of the deposition of the witnesses to be within the sphere of the normal causes of error, but not detracting from the value of the substance of the deposition itself. Finally the realization of his having to serve truth will restrain the Defender of the Bond from demanding new proofs when those already adduced are fully sufficient to establish the truth: a practice which we designated, also on another occasion, as reprehensible.

Nor should it be objected that the Defender of the Bond must write his animadversions not "pro rei veritate" but "pro validitate matrimonii." If by this is meant that the Defender of the Bond must emphasize all that favors or all that is not opposed to the existence or the continuance of the bond, the observation is indeed accurate. But if, instead, is intended the affirmation that the activity of the Defender of the Bond is not likewise bound to serve the ultimate purpose, namely, the ascertainment of the objective truth, but that he must unconditionally and independently of the proofs and results of the process sustain the imposed thesis of the existence or necessary continuance of the bond, then this assertion must be adjudged as false. Thus all those who participate in the process must without exception direct their efforts toward the sole end: "pro rei veritate!" (Doheny, *Canonical Procedure in Matrimonial Cases,* I, 1100-1101)

E. Activity

The defender may be present at the examination of the parties, witnesses and experts, and may also inspect the judicial acts at any time (C. 1678). At the hearing of the parties the defender may suggest areas of inquiry (C. 1533) and may pose questions to witnesses, though preferably through the judge (C. 1561). At the conclusion of the case the defender writes animadversions "pro vinculo et pro rei veritate" (C. 1601) and, if the case is decided in favor of nullity, the defender may appeal the decision (C. 1628).

F. Defending In Both Instances

Usually the defender in first instance and the defender in second instance are two separate people. Strictly speaking, however, the law does not require this. C. 1447 (Section A) notes that the defender in first instance may not be the *judge* or *assessor* in second instance, but says nothing about not being *defender* in second instance. Article 9 of the 1970 Instruction on Interdiocesan Tribunals (Appendix Two, p. 104) makes the same basic point. Nothing in that instruction suggests that the defender in first instance could not fulfill the same role in second instance.

ADVOCATE

A. The Pertinent Canons

C. 1481 — §1. A party can freely appoint a personal advocate and procurator; however, except for the cases stated in §§2 and 3, the party can petition and respond personally unless the judge has decided that the services of a procurator or an advocate are necessary.

§2. The accused in a penal trial must always have an advocate either appointed by the accused or given by the judge.

§3. In a contentious trial which involves minors or the public good except for marriage cases, the judge is to appoint ex officio a defender for a party who lacks one.

C. 1483 — The procurator and the advocate must have at least attained majority and be of good reputation; furthermore, the advocate must be a Catholic unless the diocesan bishop permits otherwise, must have a doctorate in canon law or be otherwise truly expert and must be approved by the same bishop.

B. Definition

An advocate is a person approved by the diocesan bishop and appointed by a party to safeguard the rights of that party by arguments regarding the law and the facts.

C. Qualities

Unlike the judge and the defender, the advocate need not have a degree in canon law. According to C.1483, however, it is required that the advocate a) be "truly expert" in canon law b) be (usually) a Catholic c) be at least eighteen years old and of good reputation and d) be approved by the bishop.

D. Appointment

An advocate is appointed not by the court but by the party. This is done by the party's signing a "mandate" commissioning a specific person to serve as his or her advocate (C. 1484).

In a marriage case it is usually only the petitioner who utilizes the service of an advocate since, in effect, the respondent's "advocate" is the defender of the bond. Should the respondent, for some reason, insist on having a personal advocate besides the defender, that would seem to be the respondent's right by reason of C. 1481. An advocate for the respondent is not, however, customary, and is, generally speaking, superfluous.

Often, indeed, even the petitioner in a marriage case foregoes, in accord with C. 1481 §1, the services of an advocate, usually on the advice of the court in those cases where it is evident early on that the marriage will easily be proved null. A court should, however, never give a negative decision without having impressed on the petitioner the importance of appointing an advocate. See page 72, D1.

E. Activities

An advocate may be present at the examination of the parties, witnesses and experts (C. 1561), may inspect the acts, etc. even though not published (C. 1678 §1, 2°), and may, of course, write a brief in favor of nullity (C. 1601).

The words of Pius XII, in his 1944 allocution to the Rota, are worth noting in this regard:

> The Advocate assists his client in drafting the preliminary "libellus" of the case, in determining rightly the object and the basis of the controversy, in expounding the salient points of the matter to be adjudicated. The Advocate points out to his client the proofs to be adduced and the documents to be produced. He suggests to his client the witnesses to be called in the case and the peremptory points to be emphasized in the deposition of the witnesses. During the trial, the Advocate assists his client justly to evaluate and to refute the exceptions and the opposing arguments. In a word, the Advocate marshals and emphasizes everything that can be alleged in favor of the petition of his client.

> In this manifold activity the Advocate may well exert every effort to win the case of his client. However, in all his activity, he must not withdraw himself from the sole and common final purpose; the discovery, the ascertainment, the legal affirmation of the truth of the objective fact. You eminent jurists and most upright Defenders of the Ecclesiastical Tribunals assembled here today, well know how the knowledge of that subordination must guide the Advocate in his reflections, in his counsels, in his arguments and in his proofs.

> You also know how this knowledge not only protects him from elaborating factitious suppositions and from accepting cases lacking in every serious basis, from employing fraud and dishonesty, from inducing the parties and the witnesses to testify falsely, from resorting to any other dishonest subterfuge, but also induces him positively to act in the whole series of acts of the process, according to the dictates of conscience. It is necessary that the work of the Advocate as well as that of the Defender of the Bond tend to the supreme triumph of truth in all its radiant splendor. For both of them, even though proceeding from opposite directions because of the different proximate ends, must of necessary tend toward the same final purpose.

> From this it is clear what must be thought of the principle unfortunately sometimes affirmed or actually followed: "The Advocate," it is said, "has the right

and the duty to effect all that benefits his thesis, just as the Defender of the Bond does in respect to the opposing thesis; for neither of the two does the norm 'Pro rei veritate' hold! The evaluation of the truth is exclusively the Judge's competency; to burden the Advocate with that task would signify thwarting or even paralyzing all his activity."

Such an assertion is based on a theoretical and practical error. It does not recognize the intimate nature and the essential final purpose of the juridical controversy. In matrimonial processes, the juridical controversy cannot be compared to a contest or a tournament in which the two contenders do not have a common final purpose, but in which each one pursues his own particular, absolute aim without respect to, and in fact, in opposition to that of his rival. In other words, each aims to defeat his adversary and carry off the victory. In this case, the winner with his recently won crown of triumph constitutes the objective fact which is to the Judge of the contest the determining motive for the awarding of the prize, because for him that is the law: To the victor belongs the prize.

The juridical contest of a matrimonial process is entirely different; for in this it is not a question of creating a fact with eloquence and dialectics but of rendering evident and giving juridical cognizance to an already existing fact. The above-mentioned principle strives to divert the work of the Advocate from the service of the objective truth and in some way would wish to attribute to skillful argumentation the creative force of law, similar to the victorious struggle in a contest. (Doheny, *Canonical Procedure in Matrimonial Cases,* I, 1102-1103)

The advocate, then, should argue pro nullitate but also pro rei veritate.

F. The Advocate And The Instructor

The roles of advocate and instructor are obviously quite different. The petitioner's *advocate* a) is appointed by the petitioner b) does not serve as a collector of evidence and c) argues with a bias in favor of the petitioner, whereas the *instructor* a) is appointed by the judge b) collects the evidence impartially and without bias and c) does not write a brief at all.

G. The Advocate And The Procurator

A procurator or proxy is one who, by legitimate mandate, performs judicial business in the name of someone else. Occasionally the person mandated to serve as advocate for the petitioner is also mandated to serve as procurator so that one and the same person would serve as Procurator-Advocate. In a marriage case, however, the petitioner generally performs personally, and not through a proxy, any judical business that need be done.

PETITIONER AND RESPONDENT

A. The Pertinent Canons

C. 1476 — Anyone, whether baptized or not, can act in a trial; however, the respondent who has been legitimately cited must answer.

C. 1477 — Although a petitioner or respondent has appointed a procurator or an advocate, they themselves are nevertheless bound to be present in person at the trial when the law or the judge prescribes it.

C. 1592 — §1. If the respondent, after having been cited, has neither appeared nor offered a suitable excuse for being absent, nor responded in accord with C. 1507 §1, the judge is to declare the respondent absent from the trial and is to decree that the case should proceed to the definitive sentence and its execution, while observing all the formalities which are to be observed.

§2. Before issuing the decree mentioned in §1, the judge must have proof that the citation drawn up by law reached the respondent within available time even by issuing a new citation if necessary.

C. 1593 — §1. If the respondent is present in court later or responds before the settlement of the case, the respondent can adduce conclusions and proofs, with due regard for the prescription of C. 1600; however, the judge is to take care that the trial is not intentionally prolonged through rather long and unnecessary delays.

§2. Even if the respondent has not appeared or responded before the settlement of the case, the respondent can use challenges against the sentence; if the respondent proves that there was a legitimate impediment for being detained which without personal fault was unable to be made known earlier, the respondent can use a complaint of nullity.

C. 1674 — The following are capable of challenging a marriage:

1° the spouses;

2° the promoter of justice when the nullity has become public, if the marriage cannot be convalidated or this is not expedient.

B. Involving The Petitioner

1. For several very good reasons no two courts operate in exactly the same way. As regards involving the petitioner, however, there are initially two basic steps (which might be called the *imparting* step and the *receiving* step) utilized by all tribunals.

2. In the *imparting* step the Tribunal conveys to the prospective petitioner at least a general outline of what lies ahead: how the process is conducted, how long it might take, what the expenses might be, etc. This is done in various ways by various Tribunals. One way of doing this is by getting into the hands of a prospective petitioner a brochure, printed in a reasonably attractive format which is both succinct enough to encourage reading and thorough enough to answer most of the questions that might occur to the average petitioner. A sample of such a brochure may be found on page 128 as Document Three.

3. In the *receiving* step the Tribunal obtains from the petitioner, either orally or in writing, either in question and answer form or in essay form, a rather complete account of the family backgrounds of the parties, their courtship, wedding, married life, separation, etc. One method (the one suggested in Document Three) of obtaining this information is by asking the prospective petitioner to complete a Marital History form. A sample of this form may be found on page 131 as Document Four.

4. When that form is received by the Tribunal and a review of it suggests that the case has potential, the Tribunal acknowledges receipt of the marital history and clarifies for the petitioner the next steps to be taken. A sample of this letter is found on page 133 as Document Five. As part of this letter the petitioner is requested at this time to sign a formal petition or libellus, a sample of which may be found on page 135 as Document Six. For more on the petition see the separate chapter on that subject on page 33.

5. At some later point, if the initial data was given in writing, an appointment is made with the petitioner for a personal interview either with the judge or with an instructor. At this interview the petitioner is asked to confirm the written account, to clarify points made in the written information and to expand on areas considered incomplete in the initial presentation.

C. Involving The Respondent

1. Once the Tribunal has accepted the libellus, it writes to the former spouse. A copy of the brochure (Document Three) if one is in use, is sent to the respondent, so that the respondent too understands the process, and the cooperation of the respondent is solicited, either by a personal interview or by a written statement (or, if need be, by telephone). A sample of a letter to the respondent (with two enclosures) may be found on page 136 as Document Seven. For more on the citation (which is the official term for this letter to the respondent) see the separate chapter on that subject on page 37.

2. The respondent must always be contacted. Only in an extremely rare case is it impossible to obtain at least some address (if only that of a relative) through which contact with the respondent can be made. In those rare cases where the respondent is absolutely unlocatable it would seem that a curator should be appointed to act in his or her stead.

3. Frequently, of course, the respondent elects not to cooperate in the proceedings. While that is certainly the respondent's right, the tribunal would do well to make it clear to the respondent at the outset that non-cooperation on his or her part will in no way prevent the tribunal from bringing the case to an affirmative decision.

D. The Absent Respondent

1. It is clear from C. 1592 that a decree of absence is issued only for the uncooperative respondent, not for the unlocatable respondent. In the case of the unlocatable respondent, as already noted, a curator should be appointed. *NB ? or ?*

2. The principal effect of the declaration of absence is that it frees the judge to proceed with the case as usual, omitting, of course, all those parts (and only those parts) which the respondent would play if he or she were present. By his or her absence the respondent is presumed to have ceded rights to all future notifications from the court except perhaps about the sentence itself.

3. C. 1593 §2, contrary to the 1917 Code (C. 1880, 8°) awards to the absent respondent the right to appeal the decision. This departure from the tenor of the 1917 law seems to play into the hands of the vindictive respondent whose only wish is to delay the case. Experience has shown that in marriage cases (which constitute nearly all the cases heard in the Church courts), some respondents, although totally disinterested in the outcome of the case as such, nevertheless wish, out of spite, to prevent the petitioner from marrying in the Church or returning to the sacraments. During the trial, therefore, they steadfastly refuse to cooperate in the hope that their silence will frustrate an affirmative decision. The present canon grants to such respondents, even though their declared absentee-ism has not been purged, i.e., shown to have been inculpable, the right to appeal, which in practice will often delay the case further by involving the court in full appellate procedures rather than simple ratification. The bona fide rights of respondents should of course be scrupulously guarded by the law, but this particular ruling seems to be a case of misplaced concern. *How VERY TRUE* *but the slip-shod boys brought it all on!*

E. The Delcarations Of The Parties

Regarding the declarations of the parties, that is, their formal testimony, see the separate chapter on that topic on page 41.

F. Respondent As Co-Petitioner

Occasionally the "other party" is just as eager to obtain a declaration of nullity as the petitioner is and so wishes to act as a co-petitioner. Sometimes, furthermore, the other party feels disadvantaged by being labeled "the respondent." Since the court (unlike many lay people) does not see either the petitioner or the respondent as a "favored" person, and since, therefore, it is, generally speaking, a matter of indifference to the court which party in a marriage case acts as petitioner, the court, it would seem, could permit *both* parties to petition for the declaration. In that case, however, both parties would also have to be considered co-respondents since C. 1620, 4° requires that, for a valid trial, there must always be a respondent (pars conventa).

A. The Pertinent Canons

C. 1478 — §1. Minors and those who lack the use of reason can stand trial only through their parents or guardians or curators, with due regard for the prescription of §3.

§2. If the judge decides that the rights of minors are in conflict with the rights of the parents, guardians or curators, or that the latter cannot satisfactorily safeguard the rights of the former, then they are to be represented in the trial by a guardian or curator appointed by the judge.

§3. But in spiritual cases and in cases connected with spiritual matters, if minors have attained the use of reason, they can act and respond without the consent of parents or guardian; if they have completed their fourteenth year of age, they can do so on their own; if not, through a curator appointed by the judge.

§4. Those deprived of the administration of their goods and those who are of diminished mental capacity can stand trial personally only to answer for their own offenses or at the prescription of the judge; in all other cases they must act and respond through their curators.

C. 1479— Whenever a guardian or curator appointed by civil authority is present, this person can be admitted by an ecclesiastical judge after having heard the diocesan bishop of the person to whom the guardian or curator has been given, if this can be done; but if a guardian or curator is not present or does not appear admissible, the judge shall designate a guardian or curator for the case.

B. Definition Of Terms

A guardian or curator is a person appointed or accepted by the court to safeguard the rights of another person (called the "ward") and to represent that person at trial primarily in those instances where the ward is either a minor or of diminished mental capacity.

Preferably the term "guardian" is used when the ward is under age, and the term "curator" when the ward is of diminished mental capacity. In practice, however, the terms are used interchangeably.

C. Use Of Curator Or Guardian

Although the law does not state clearly exactly when a curator or guardian should be appointed, it would seem that there are four principal instances in which this should be done:

1. *When the respondent is a minor.* This, of course, is rare in a marriage case.

2. *When the respondent either lacks the use of reason altogether or is weak-minded.* The question might arise here: does the phrase "those who are of diminished mental capacity" include all those who are listed in C. 1095, namely, those who lack the due reason, discretion, or competence for marriage? The answer seems clearly to be *no.* A respondent, for example, whose severe personality disorder deprived him or her of the capacity to enter a marital covenant is not necessarily deprived, by that disorder, of the capacity to enter a non-marital type of contract, or to conduct his or her own legal or judicial affairs. Few people who suffer from personality disorders are appropriately referred to as "those who are of diminished mental capacity," i.e., "ii qui minus firmae mentis sunt." Therefore, not all those respondents in marriage cases, whose marital incompetence is alleged, need have guardians appointed for them, but only those who either lack the use of reason altogether or are weak minded.

3. *When the respondent can in no way be located.* As noted in the previous chapter, this occurs only very rarely. When in fact it does occur, however, it seems appropriate and in accord with the general principles of law, that a guardian be appointed.

4. *When the respondent is judged to be dangerous and threatening.* Occasionally the petitioner will provide the court with an address for the respondent but plead with the court to hear the case without notifying the respondent because, should the respondent learn of the action, he or she would be likely to cause physical harm to the petitioner. Such a request should be granted only rarely and then only after careful investigation but there are unquestionably some cases where the grant is justified.

D. Time Of Appointment

The appointment of a curator or guardian should be made early on in the proceedings since at the very beginning of the case it is the curator or guardian, not the respondent, who is cited (see the chapter on the citation on page 39 and specifically C. 1508 §3) in all those cases in which a guardian or curator is required.

32

PETITION

A. The Pertinent Canons

C. 1501 — A judge cannot adjudicate any case unless the party concerned or the promoter of justice has presented a petition in accord with the norm of the canons.

C. 1502 — A person who wishes to bring another to court must present a *libellus* to a competent judge, which explains the object of the controversy and requests the services of the judge.

C. 1503 — §1. The judge may accept an oral petition if either the petitioner is impeded from presenting a *libellus* or the case can be easily investigated and is of lesser importance.

§2. But in either situation the judge is to require the notary to put the act into writing, which is to be read to and approved by the petitioner; this then takes the place of and has all the legal effects of a *libellus* written by the petitioner.

C. 1504 — A *libellus* which introduces a suit must:

1° express before which judge the case is being introduced, what is being petitioned and by whom the petition is being made;

2° indicate the basis for the petitioner's right and at least in general the facts and proofs which will be used to prove what has been alleged;

3° be signed by the petitioner or procurator, adding the day, month and year, as well as the address of the petitioner or procurator or the place where they say they reside for the purpose of receiving the acts;

4° indicate the domicile or quasi-domicile of the respondent.

C. 1505 — §1. After the single judge or the president of a collegiate tribunal has recognized both that the matter is within his competence and that the petitioner does not lack legitimate personal standing in court, he must accept or reject the *libellus* as soon as possible through a decree.

§2. A *libellus* can be rejected only:

1° if the judge or the tribunal is incompetent;

2° if it is undoubtedly clear that the petitioner lacks legitimate personal standing in court;

3° if the prescriptions of C. 1504, nn. 1-3 have not been observed;

4° if from the *libellus* itself it is certainly obvious that it lacks any basis whatsoever and that it is impossible that any such basis would appear through a process.

§3. If the *libellus* has been rejected due to defects which can be corrected, the petitioner can properly draw up a new *libellus* and again present it to the same judge.

§4. A party is always free within ten available days (*tempus utile*) to lodge a reasoned recourse against the rejection of the *libellus* before the appellate tribunal or the college if it had been rejected by its president; the question of the rejection is to be resolved as quickly as possible.

C. 1506 — If within a month from the presentation of the *libellus* the judge has not issued a decree by which he accepts or rejects the *libellus* in accord with the norm of C. 1505, the interested party can insist that the judge fulfill his duty; but if the judge, nevertheless, remains silent for ten days after the petitioner's insistence, the petition is considered as having been accepted.

B. The Terms: Libellus And Petition

The Latin word *libellus* means "a little book" or "something in writing." When that something in writing was a slanderous calumny, it was known as a *libellus famosus* and was, precisely because it was in writing, considered a more serious crime than oral slander. In English law, it came to be known simply as *libel*. When, on the other hand, the something in writing was a request made of a judge to hear a case, it was known as a *libellus litis introductorius* or, as we might say in English, the introductory bill of complaint. It is in this latter sense that the term *libellus* is used here.

The *libellus* is commonly referred to simply as the petition, though strictly speaking, canon law still regards the judicial petition as a generic term which includes two types: the written type called the *libellus,* and the oral type called the oral petition.

C. Contents Of A Petition

1. C. 1504, 2° says that a petition which introduces a suit must indicate the basis (quo iure) for the petitioner's right and, at least in general, the facts and proofs (quibus factis et probationibus) which will be used to prove what has been alleged.

2. This means that the character of a petition is non-probatory but that, nevertheless, two things must be indicated: a) the basis and b) the method to be followed later in proving the allegations (the via argumentationis).

3. This establishes what is called the "fumus boni iuris," the semblance of a well founded right, or what might be called "probable cause."

4. In those courts which require a Marital History to be completed and reviewed prior to a formal petition, the petition itself is usually a very simple, direct request worded somewhat as follows: I, John Jones, hereby request the tribunal of the Diocese of _____ to declare null my marriage to Mary Smith on the grounds of _____ in accord with my Marital History. See Document Six on page 135.

In those courts which do not use a Marital History the petition would be somewhat longer and would have to indicate, in accord with C. 1504, 2°, the basis, the facts and the proofs.

D. Reasons For Rejecting A Petition

1. C. 1505 §2, 3° and 4° notes that a petition can be rejected only:

    a. if it fails to state either the basis (quo iure) or, in general, the facts and proofs (quibus factis et probationibus) — or

    b. if it is clear from the petition itself that the request lacks any foundation and that none could materialize during the course of a trial.

2. The canon, therefore, indicates that there are three substantial reasons for rejecting a petition:

    a. *No basis* — as, for example, when the grounds alleged for nullity are not recognized grounds, e.g. sterility.

    b. *No proofs* — as, for example, when the grounds are recognized, e.g. impotence, but are totally non-demonstrable because the allegedly impotent party will not cooperate and the matter has always been kept an absolute secret.

    c. *No foundation* — as, for example, when the grounds are recognized, e.g. impotence, but are certainly false in the marriage in question, from which, say, five children were born, with the woman claiming never to have been unfaithful.

E. The Procedure in Rejecting A Petition

1. C. 1505 §1 notes that when the court (either a single judge, a college, or the president of the college) concludes that a petition is substantially deficient as indicated above, it should reject the petition by decree. The decree, in accord with C. 1617, should state, at least summarily, the reasons for the rejection.

2. C. 1505 § 4 notes that a party is always free to interpose within ten days a recourse, which contains the reasons against the rejection of the petition, either to the appellate tribunal or to the college, if the petition has been rejected by its president.

3. Should the petitioner, in accord with §4, have recourse to the appellate tribunal and that tribunal finds the rejection unwarranted, the procedure then is for the appellate tribunal not to hear the case, but rather to remand the case to the lower tribunal for acceptance of petition and hearing.

CITATION AND JOINDER OF ISSUES

A. The Pertinent Canons

C. 1507 — §1. In the decree which accepts the *libellus* of the petitioner the judge or president must either call into court or cite the other parties for the joinder of issues (*contestatio litis*), determining whether they must respond in writing or present themselves personally before the judge in order to join the issues. But if from the written responses the judge perceives that it is necessary to call the parties together for a session, that can be determined in a new decree.

C. 1508 — §1. The decree of citation to the trial must be forwarded immediately to the respondent and at the same time to others who are to appear.

§2. The introductory *libellus* is to be joined to the citation unless for serious reasons the judge determines that the *libellus* is not to be made known to the respondent before the latter makes a deposition during the trial.

§3. If the suit is filed against a person who does not have the free exercise of personal rights or the free administration of the controverted items, the citation is to be made known to the guardian, curator or special procurator, as the case may be, or to the person who is bound to enter the trial in the respondent's name according to the norm of law.

C. 1509 — §1. Notification of citations, decrees, sentences and other judicial acts are to be made in accordance with the norms determined in particular law through the public postal services or through another method which is the safest.

§2. The fact and method of notification must be clear in the acts.

C. 1510 — A respondent who refuses to accept the document of citation or who prevents its arrival is considered as having been legitimately cited.

C. 1511 - If the citation has not been legitimately communicated, the acts of the process are null, with due regard for the prescription of C. 1507 §3.

C. 1512 — Once the citation has been legitimately communicated or the parties have appeared before the judge to pursue the case:

1° the issue ceases to be *res integra;*

2° the case becomes proper to that judge or tribunal before whom the action was begun and is competent in other respects;

3° the jurisdiction of a delegated judge is firmly established so that it does not expire when the right of the one delegating ceases;

4° prescription is interrupted unless otherwise provided;

5° the litigation begins to be pending and therefore the principle becomes operative: *while a suit is pending, nothing new is to be introduced.*

C. 1513 — §1. The joinder of issues (*contestatio litis*) occurs when the terms of the controversy based on the petitions and responses of the parties are specified by the decree of the judge.

§2. The petitions and responses of the parties, besides those in the *libellus* introducing the suit, can be expressed either in response to the citation or in a declaration made orally before the judge; in more difficult cases, however, the parties are to be called together by the judge to specify the question or questions to be answered in the sentence.

§3. The decree of the judge is to be made known to the parties; unless they have already reached an agreement, they can within ten days make recourse to that judge that it be changed; however, the issue is to be resolved as quickly as possible by a decree of that judge.

C. 1514 — Once the terms of the controversy have been determined, they cannot validly be changed except for a serious reason through a new decree at the request of one party and after hearing the other parties and considering their reasons.

C. 1515 — Once the joinder of issues (*contestatio litis*) has occurred, the possessor of another's property ceases to be in good faith; if therefore, the possessor is sentenced to make restitution, the profits made from the day of the joinder of issues (*contestatio litis*) must also be returned and any damages compensated.

C. 1516 — Once the joinder of issues (*contestatio litis*) has occurred, the judge is to furnish the parties suitable time to present and complete proofs.

C. 1677 — §1. When the *libellus* has been accepted, the presiding judge or the *ponens* is to proceed to the communication of the decree of citation according to the norms of C. 1508.

§2. Unless either party has petitioned for a session on the joinder of the issues (*contestatio litis*), when fifteen days have passed after such a communication, the presiding judge or the *ponens* is to determine the formulation of the doubt or doubts within ten days by a decree ex officio and notify the parties.

§3. The formulation of the doubt not only is to ask whether there is proof of nullity of marriage in the case, but it also must determine on what ground or grounds the validity of the marriage is to be challenged.

§4. Ten days after the communication of the decree, the presiding judge or the *ponens* is to arrange for the instruction of the case by a new decree if the parties were not opposed.

B. The Citation

1. *Description*

In general the citation is defined as the judicial summons apprising the respondent (or the respondent's guardian or curator) of the petition, and calling for a written response to the petitioner's claim.

In practice the citation is the letter to the respondent already discussed on page 28. A sample of that letter is found on page 136 as Document Seven.

In accord with C. 1508 §2, the judge customarily orders that a copy of the libellus *not* be enclosed in the letter citing the respondent.

2. *The Person Cited*

Generally it is the respondent in person who is cited. As noted on page 32, however, and in accord with C. 1508 §3, the guardian or curator is cited rather than the respondent in the following cases: when the respondent is a minor, when the whereabouts of the respondent are completely unknown, when the respondent is weak-minded, and when the respondent is dangerous.

3. *The Effects of the Citation*

C. 1512 notes that, with the citation, the trial officially opens and the case becomes proper to the tribunal before which the action was begun.

This means, for example, that if a marital history were received and approved by a tribunal competent only by reason of the respondent's domicile, in the event that the respondent moved, that tribunal would lose jurisdiction if the move occured *before* the citation but would retain it if the move was *after* the citation.

C. The Joinder Of Issues

1. *Description*

In general the joinder of issues is the defining of the terms of the controversy (based on the petitioner's libellus and the other party's response) by the decree of the judge.

In practice the decree is very brief, and states the issue in the form of a question. In Latin the traditional phrase is: An constet de nullitate matrimonii Buzzard-Quail ob caput _____ . In English, it may be phrased as follows: Whether the Buzzard-Quail marriage has been proved null on the grounds of _____ .

2. Establishing the Ground

Oftentimes a marriage may be proved null on several grounds. Generally speaking, however, it is helpful, from the point of view both of investigating the facts and of writing the sentence, to establish one single, precise ground on which the case will be judged, e.g. an intention against children on the part of the respondent, lack of due discretion on the part of the petitioner, force and fear imposed on the petitioner.

3. Changing the Ground

C. 1514 is quite clear in stating that, once the terms of the controversy are determined, they cannot easily be changed. The "terms of the controversy" in a marriage case, however, would appear to refer to the basic issue of whether or not invalidity has been proved. The "terms of the controversy" in other words, are not at all synonymous with the "ground."

In practice, indeed, minor changes in the *ground* are routinely made by the judge. Lack of due competence, for example, may be changed during the course of the trial to lack of due discretion. This sort of change is justified either by the fact that such a minor, technical change is not a real but only a logical change, or by noting that many rotal decisions have recognized quite disparate grounds (lack of due discretion, for example, and an intention against children) as equivalently concordant. See, for example, SRRD, 66, 340-341.

4. Notifying the Parties

C. 1513 §3 and C. 1677 §§3 and 4 indicate that both parties should be apprised of the ground, a requirement not presently met by all American tribunals.

DECLARATIONS AND CONFESSIONS OF THE PARTIES

A. The Pertinent Canons

C. 1530 — The Judge can always interrogate the parties so as to reveal the truth more effectively; in fact the judge must do so at the request of a party or to prove a fact which is to be established beyond doubt for the sake of the public interest. *(marriage cases)*

C. 1531 — §1. A party legitimately interrogated must answer and tell the whole truth.

§2. But if a party has refused to answer, it is for the judge to evaluate what can be drawn from that refusal concerning the proof of the facts.

C. 1532 — Unless a serious cause persuades otherwise, the judge is to administer an oath to the parties to tell the truth or at least to confirm the truth of their testimony in cases where the public good is at stake; the judge, in accord with prudential judgment, can do the same in other cases.

C. 1533 — The parties, the promoter of justice and the defender of the bond can present to the judge items on which a party is to be interrogated.

C. 1534 - To the extent it is possible the regulations of cc 1548, §2, n.1, 1552 and 1558-1565 on witnesses are to be observed in the interrogation of the parties.

C. 1535 — A judicial confession is a written or oral assertion against oneself made by any party regarding the matter under trial and made before a competent judge, whether spontaneously or upon interrogation by the judge.

C. 1536 — §1. If it is a question of some private matter and the public good is not at stake the judicial confession of one party relieves the other parties from the burden of proof.

§2. In cases which concern the public good, however, a judicial confession and the declarations of the parties which are not confessions can have a probative force to be evaluated by the judge along with the other circumstances of the case; but complete probative force cannot be attributed to them unless other elements are present which thoroughly corroborate them. *indicia, adminicula ;~*

C. 1537 — Having weighed all the circumstances, it is for the judge to evaluate the worth of an extra-judicial confession which has been introduced into the trial.

C. 1538 — A confession or any other declaration of a party lacks all probative force if it is proved that it was made through an error of fact or it was extorted by force or grave fear.

B. The Form Of Judicial Declarations And Confessions

1. The *petitioner* usually makes his or her declaration and/or confession before a judge or an instructor. In those tribunals where the principal account of the petitioner is made by completing a Marital History Form, the petitioner will be asked to incorporate that account into the judicial proceedings by confirming it under oath at the hearing. During the remainder of the hearing the auditor will then ask the petitioner to clarify or amplify areas that were not sufficiently clear or detailed in the Marital History. In those tribunals where a Marital History is not used, the formal hearing of the petitioner will usually be longer and more wide-ranging.

2. The *respondent's* declaration and/or confession is made in whatever way the respondent chooses to do so. Preferably, of course, it is done by the respondent's appearance before the judge or instructor. Often, however, the respondent declines to do that, in which case C. 1528 suggests that the services of a Designated Receiver may be used, or an affidavit may be obtained from the respondent, or the respondent's observations may be obtained "in any other legitimate manner." In practice a respondent will often consent only to converse on the telephone.

C. Distinction Between Confession And Declaration

1. *Definitions*

   a. Confession. A confession, in general, is a written or oral assertion against oneself (contra se) made by a party regarding the matter under trial. When it is made before a judge it is called a judicial confession; when it is made outside the tribunal setting it is called an extrajudicial confession. A confession in a marriage case is somewhat different from one made in a penal case, because in a marriage case it is often not a confession in the true or strict sense since it is not really contra se. In a penal case the issue at bar involves a crime. If the accused confesses to that crime, that is truly contra se and involves some sanction or penalty. In a marriage case, however, a party often "confesses" not so much to a crime as simply to being human and to certain human failings.

   b. Declaration. A declaration is a statement by a party that is in no way self accusatory.

2. *Distinction*

   Basically a *confession* is in some way self accusatory (a respondent, for example, might confess that she intended to exclude children, or a petitioner might confess that he drank to excess) whereas a *declaration* is in no way self accusatory (a petitioner, for example, might claim that the respondent denied him children, or the respondent might claim that the petitioner drank to excess).

42

D. Distinction Between Petitioner And Respondent

The unintiated might think that the petitioner makes a declaration whereas the respondent makes a confession. In fact it does not necessarily work that way. Often, for example, a petitioner might claim that he or she lacked due discretion in entering marriage and so might "confess" to having been, at the time of marriage, imprudent, rebellious, irresponsible and abusing drugs. In such a case the respondent will be asked to testify or "declare" not about himself or herself but rather about the petitioner.

E. Probative Force Of Declaration Or Confession

In general it is perhaps true that a confession is a bit more credible than a declaration. At another level, however, it is important to bear in mind that the accounts offered by the petitioner and respondent are a product of a lifetime of character building. People are more or less perceptive, tolerant, bitter, charitable, broad minded, self serving, philosophical, psychological, vindictive, etc. etc. Oftentimes the account given to the tribunal is an amalgam of declarations and confessions that is more credible in one place than in another. The account also reflects, as a rule, the ability of the person to communicate (which no doubt reflects the communication skills utilized by the person within the context of the marriage).

The question of credibility is, then, a complex one. In light of this complexity, canons 1536 §2 and 1537 wisely and admirably leave the matter of the probative force of both judicial and extrajudicial assertions of the parties to the evaluation (aestimatio) of the judge.

Always, or almost always, of course, the judge will make that evaluation in light of the observations made by the affiants and witnesses.

A. C. 1540 — §1. Public ecclesiastical documents are those which official persons have drawn up in the exercise of their function in the Church, after having observed the formalities prescribed by law.

§2. Public civil documents are those which are considered to be such in law in accord with the laws of the individual place.

§3. Other documents are private ones.

NB. Most of our "depositions" are such

C. 1541 — Unless contrary and evident arguments show otherwise, public documents are to be trusted concerning everything which is directly and principally affirmed in them.

C. 1542 — A private document whether acknowledged by a party or recognized by the judge has the same probative force against its author or signer and those deriving a case from them as does an extra-judicial confession; against outsiders it has the same force as the declarations of the parties which are not confessions, in accord with the norm of C. 1536 §2.

NB Discussing of the genuineness of some... to ping him and to counsel for...

C. 1543 — If the documents are shown to have been erased, corrected, interpolated, or affected by another such defect, it is for the judge to assess whether such documents have value and how much. *ask for this*

C. 1544 — Documents do not have probative force in a trial unless they are originals or presented in authentic copy and are deposited with the chancery of the tribunal so that they may be examined by the judge and the opposing party.

C. 1545 — The judge can order that a document which is common to both parties be exhibited in the process.

C. 1546 §1. Even if documents are common, no one is obliged to exhibit those which cannot be communicated without risk of harm in accordance with the norm of C. 1548 §2, n. 2 or without risk of violating the obligation to observe secrecy.

way to BB!

§2. Nonetheless, if some excerpt, at least, of a document can be transcribed and can be presented in copy form without the above-mentioned hazards the judge can decree that it be produced.

B. Definitions

An affiant is a person who makes an affidavit.

An affidavit is a statement made before a notary and confirmed by oath or solemn affirmation.

If it is not taken by an auditor duly assigned, only made before a notary. (non judicial) it is a document when written up.

44

In canon law an affidavit is regarded as a document.

In practice the affidavit is completed by a person named by one of the parties as someone who would be knowledgeable about the parties, their courtship, marriage and separation. The judge writes a letter to all such people asking usually for fairly detailed information. A sample of such a letter may be found as Document Eight on page 139.

C. Probative Force Of Affidavit

William Doheny, in his book *Canonical Procedure in Matrimonial Cases* (Vol. I, p. 400) says the following regarding the probative force of an affidavit:

> In English-speaking countries affidavits are frequently resorted to as a means of documentary proof or evidence. These affidavits are written declarations or statements confirmed by oath or solemn affirmation. Since they are oftentimes presented in marriage cases, judges and other officers of the court should be warned not to ascribe to them more probative force than they purport to carry. An affidavit merely certifies that a specific person made a solemn affirmation confirmed by oath before a duly qualified notary public at a certain time. Obviously, such a statement, in itself, even though under oath does not constitute full proof in matrimonial cases. The inherent truth of the statement and the facts attested must be further investigated.

D. Confidentiality

1. *Of the affidavit*

It would appear that a potential affiant could, in accord with C. 1546 and C. 1598, issue an affidavit with an assurance from the judge that the affidavit will never be published "in order to avoid very serious dangers." If, however, the affidavit is issued without that request for confidentiality, it would be subject to the usual publication along with the rest of the evidence.

2. *Of the affiant*

In the chapter of the Code on witnesses, it is required (C. 1554) that the names of all witnesses be communicated to the parties. In this chapter on affiants, however, no such requirement is made. The names of the affiants, therefore, need not be communicated to the parties.

E. The Credibility Of Affiants

C. 1572 and C. 1573 on the credibility of *witnesses* applies equally to the credibility of *affiants*. C. 1572 notes that the moral, mental, material and numerical criteria must all be weighed by the judge in deciding how much credence to give to the observations of a given person. C. 1573 notes that, generally speaking, the statements of a single individual do not result in full proof. See pages 51-53.

WITNESSES

A. The Pertinent Canons

The Code contains twenty-seven canons on Witnesses and Testimony. All twenty-seven are pertinent and are therefore reprinted here along with their four article headings. They begin with two introductory canons:

C. 1547 — Proof by means of witnesses is admitted in every kind of case under the supervision of the judge.

C. 1548 — §1. When the judge legitimately interrogates witnesses they must tell the truth.

§2. With due regard for the prescription of C. 1550 §2, n. 2, the following are exempted from the obligation to answer:

1° clerics in regard to whatever was made known to them in connection with their sacred ministry; civil officials, doctors, obstetricians, advocates, notaries and others who are bound to professional secrecy, even by reason of advice rendered, as regards matters subject to this secrecy;

2° persons who fear that infamy, dangerous vexations or other serious evils will happen to themselves, or their spouse, or persons related to them by consanguinity or affinity, as a result of their testimony.

Art. 1
THOSE WHO CAN BE WITNESSES

C. 1549 — All persons can be witnesses unless they are expressly excluded by law, either completely or partially.

C. 1550 — §1. Minors below the fourteenth year of age and those who are feebleminded are not allowed to give testimony; however, they may be heard by reason of a decree of the judge which declares such a hearing expedient.

§2. The following are considered incapable:

1° those who are parties in the case, or who represent the parties in the trial; the judge and assistants, the advocate and others who are assisting or have assisted the parties in the same case;

2° priests as regards everything which has become known to them by reason of sacramental confession, even if the penitent requests their manifestation; moreover, whatever has been heard by anyone or in any way on the occasion of confession cannot be accepted as even an indication of the truth.

Art. 2
THE INTRODUCTION AND EXCLUSION OF WITNESSES

C. 1551 — The party who has introduced a witness can forego the examination of the witness; but the opposing party can demand that the witness be examined notwithstanding that action.

C. 1552 — °1. When proof by means of witnesses is demanded, their names and domicile are to be made known to the tribunal.

§2. The items of discussion upon which interrogation of the witnesses is sought are to be presented within the time limit set by the judge; otherwise the petition is to be considered as abandoned.

C. 1553 — It is the judge's responsibility to curb an excessive number of witnesses.

C. 1554 — Before witnesses are examined, their names are to be made known to the parties; however, if in the prudent assessment of the judge, that cannot be done without serious difficulty, it is to be done at least before the publication of the testimony.

C. 1555 — With due regard for the prescription of C. 1550, a party can request that a witness be excluded if a just cause for exclusion is demonstrated before the interrogation of the witness.

C. 1556 — The citation of a witness is done by a decree of the judge made known to the witness according to law.

C. 1557 — A witness who has been duly cited is to appear or inform the judge of the reason for the absence.

Art. 3
THE EXAMINATION OF WITNESSES

C. 1558 — §1. Witnesses must be examined at the tribunal unless it appears otherwise appropriate to the judge.

§2. Cardinals, patriarchs, bishops and those who, by the law of their state, enjoy a similar right, are to be heard in a place which they themselves select.

§3. The judge is to decide where those are to be heard for whom it is impossible or difficult to come to the tribunal because of distance, illness or other impediment with due regard for the prescriptions of C. 1418 and C. 1469 §2.

C. 1559 — The parties may not assist in the examination of witnesses unless the judge believes that they must be admitted, especially when the matter concerns the private good. On the other hand, their advocates or their procurators may assist unless the judge believes that the process must be carried on in secret because of the circumstances of things or persons.

C. 1560 — §1. Each of the witnesses must be examined individually.

§2. If the witnesses disagree among themselves or with a party in a serious matter the judge can bring them together or have them come to an agreement with one another, precluding disputes and scandal insofar as it is possible.

C. 1561 — The examination of a witness is conducted by the judge, a delegate or an auditor, who is to be assisted by a notary; as a result, if the parties, or the promoter of justice, or the defender of the bond, or the advocates who are present at the examination have further questions to be put to the witness, they are to propose these questions not to the witness but to the judge or the person taking the judge's place who is to ask them, unless particular law provides otherwise.

C. 1562 — §1. The judge is to call to the attention of the witness the serious obligation to tell the whole truth and only the truth.

§2. The judge is to administer the oath to the witness in accord with C. 1532; but the witness who refuses to take it is to be heard without the oath.

C. 1563 — The judge, first of all, is to establish the identity of the witness; the judge should seek out what is the relationship of the witness with the parties, and, when addressing specific questions to the witness regarding the case, the judge is also to inquire about the sources of the witness' knowledge and the precise time the witness learned what is asserted.

C. 1564 — The questions are to be brief, accommodated to the intelligence of the person being interrogated, not comprising several points at the same time, not captious, nor crafty, nor suggestive of the answer, free from every kind of offense and pertinent to the case being tried.

C. 1565 — §1. The questions must not be communicated to the witnesses ahead of time.

§2. However, if the matters which are to be testified to are so removed from memory that unless they are recalled earlier they cannot be affirmed with certainty, the judge may advise the witness of some matters if it is thought that this can be done without danger.

C. 1566 — Witnesses are to give testimony orally; they are not to read from written memoranda, unless there is question of calculation and accounts; in such a case they may consult the notes which they brought with them.

C. 1567 — §1. The answer is to be put in writing at once by the notary who must report the exact words of the testimony given, at least as regards those points which touch directly upon the matter of the trial.

§2. Use of a tape recorder is allowed provided that, afterwards, the answers are transcribed and are signed by those making the depositions, if possible.

C. 1568 — The notary is to make mention in the acts whether the oath was taken, omitted, or refused, also of the presence of the parties and of other persons, the questions added ex officio and, in general, everything noteworthy which may have occurred while the witnesses were being examined.

C. 1569 — §1. At the conclusion of the examination what the notary has put in writing from the deposition must be read to the witness or the witness must be given an opportunity to listen to the tape recording of the deposition with the option of adding to, suppressing, correcting or changing it.

§2. Finally, the acts must be signed by the witness, the judge and the notary.

C. 1570 — Although witnesses have already been examined, they can be recalled for another examination at the request of a party or ex officio but before the acts or the testimony have been published; this is true if the judge believes such a reexamination necessary or useful, provided, however, that there is no danger of collusion or corruption.

C. 1571 — In accord with an equitable assessment of the judge, witnesses must be compensated both for the expenses they have incurred and for the income they have lost by rendering testimony.

Art. 4
THE TRUSTWORTHINESS OF TESTIMONIES

C. 1572 — In evaluating testimony, after having obtained testimonial letters if need be, the judge should consider;

1° the condition and good reputation of the person;

2° whether the witness testifies in virtue of personal knowledge, expecially what has been seen and heard personally, or whether the testimony is the witness' opinion, or a rumor or hearsay from others;

3° whether the witness is reliable and firmly consistent or rather inconsistent, uncertain or vacillating;

4° whether the witness has supporting witnesses or whether there is support from other sources of proof.

50

C. 1573 — The deposition of a single witness cannot constitute full proof unless a witness acting in an official capacity makes a deposition regarding duties performed ex officio or unless circumstances of things and persons suggest otherwise.

B. Etymology Of Terms

1. The English word *wit/ness* is a compound word (like gover/ness or high/ness) which means a person having wit or knowledge—not just speculative knowledge but knowledge that comes from one or more of the five senses, or five wits, as they have been called. The German word *wissen* is also a member of this family.

2. The English word *testimony* (and the Latin word *testis* which means both "testicle" and "witness") derives, no doubt, from the Abrahamic oath ritual in which the patriarch instructed the swearer "place your hand under my thigh" as recorded in Genesis 24:2 and 47:29. *The Jerome Biblical Commentary* (24) notes that "Swearing by the genital organs, considered the transmitters of life, added solemnity to the oath."

C. Definitions

1. *Witness.* A witness is one who, having been summoned by the court, responds, usually under oath, to the questions posed by the judge, auditor or designated receiver, in a matter pending before the court.

2. *Testimony.* Testimony is the deposition given, usually under oath, by a witness to a judge or to the judge's locum tenens and recorded either by a notary or by a tape recorder.

D. Confidentiality Of Witnesses

1. C. 1554 notes that the *names* of all witnesses are to be made known to the parties before they actually give testimony or at least prior to the publication of the acts.

2. According to C. 1678 §2, however, the parties may not be present at the actual hearing of the witnesses in a marriage case.

E. Credibility Of Witnesses

1. C. 1572 instructs the judge, in evaluating the credence that should be given to individual witnesses, to look to four criteria:

   1° the *moral* criteria, i.e. the honesty and good reputation of the person.

   2° the *mental* criteria, i.e. whether the information offered by the witness is personal knowledge or whether it is only opinion, rumor or hearsay.

3° the *material* criteria, i.e. whether the witness is consistent or inconsistent.

4° the *numerical* criteria, i.e. whether this witness and the others are

    a. concordant - i.e. in total agreement

    b. cumulative - i.e. in general agreement though differing in specifics

    c. diversative - i.e. referring to different matters altogether

    d. adversative - i.e. repugnant

2. Although the judge should be alert to all four of these criteria (the moral, mental, material and numerical) and their shades of actual presence in witnesses, perhaps a special word is in order regarding the *numerical* criteria. Most witnesses in marriage cases are a combination of concordant, cumulative, diversative and adversative, i.e. part of their testimony tells of events related by other witnesses in substantially the same or somewhat different way; part of their testimony refers to events apparently unknown by the other witnesses or related differently; and sometimes their observations about the same event are quite contradictory.

   The rule of thumb for evaluating such testimony is as follows:

   a. concordant testimony is probative

   b. cumulative testimony is corroborative

   c. diversative testimony is neutral

   d. adversative testimony is vitiating

3. On this same criterion, the numerical criterion, it bears noting that, according to C. 1573, even though, generally speaking, the testimony of a single witness does not result in full proof, still, in a given case, a judge might conclude that a matter is proven by a single testimony plus other circumstances.

F. Witnesses And Affiants

Most courts these days tend, generally speaking, to procure affidavits rather than testimony.

This is partly perhaps because the names of *affiants* need not be made known to the parties whereas the names of *witnesses* must be. But mostly it is because the taking of testimony is far more time consuming than the procuring of an affidavit. Given the limited personnel in most courts, this is an important factor.

52

It is perhaps true that well taken testimony is often a bit more thorough than an affidavit received from the same person. But it is also true that, given the time involved, a court tends to limit the number of testimonies taken, whereas, because of the ease with which they can be obtained, the number of affidavits are never or almost never restricted. In practice, therefore, a court, generally speaking, obtains more information through affidavits than it does through testimonies.

EXPERTS

A. The Pertinent Canons

C. 1574 — The services of experts must be used whenever their examination and opinion, based on the laws of art or science, are required in order to establish some fact or to clarify the true nature of some thing by reason of a prescription of the law or a judge.

C. 1575 — It is the responsibility of the judge either to name experts after listening to the parties and the names they propose, or to make use of reports, if warranted, already drawn up by other experts.

C. 1576 — Experts can be excluded or rejected for the same reasons that witnesses can be.

C. 1577 — §1. After paying attention to those points which may have been brought forward by the litigants, the judge is to specify by a decree the individual points on which the expert's services must focus.

§2. The acts of the case and other documents and aids which the expert may need in order to function properly and faithfully must be turned over to the expert.

§3. After listening to the expert, the judge should fix the time within which the examination is to be carried out and the report presented.

C. 1578 — §1. Each of the experts should draw up a report distinct from the others unless the judge orders that one report be made and signed by the experts individually; if this latter is done, differences of opinion, if any, are to be carefully noted.

§2. The experts must indicate clearly by what documents or other apt means they have been informed about the identity of persons, things or places, by what path and method they proceeded in discharging the function given to them and on what grounds, for the most part, their conclusions are based.

§3. An expert can be summoned by the judge to supply further explanations which may seem necessary.

C. 1579 — §1. The judge is to weigh attentively not only the conclusions of the experts, even when they are concordant, but also the other circumstances of the case.

§2. In giving the reasons for the decision, the judge must express what considerations prompted him or her to admit or reject the conclusions of the experts.

C. 1580 — Both the expenses and the stipends which must be paid to the experts are to be determined justly and equitably by the judge with due regard for particular law.

C. 1581 — §1. The parties may designate private experts who must be approved by the judge.

§2. If the judge admits them, they may inspect the acts of the case if necessary and be present at the discharging of the court experts' function; moreover they can always present their own report.

C. 1680 — In cases of impotence or defect of consent due to mental illness, the judge is to use the services of one or more experts unless it is obvious from the circumstances that this would be useless; in other cases the prescription of C. 1574 is to be observed.

B. Definition

An expert is a specialist who is learned, experienced, and skilled in his or her science or profession and whose scientific report is required either to prove some fact or to diagnose the true nature of something.

The term "expert" refers most often to psychiatrists, psychologists and others in the field of mental health, though it may also refer, in impotence cases, to urologists and gynecologists.

C. Necessity Of An Expert

C. 1680 indicates that the services of an expert should be used 1) in cases of impotence or defect of consent 2) due to mental illness 3) unless involvement of an expert would be useless 4), or it might be added (though the canon does not mention this), unless it would be impossible to obtain the services of an expert.

1. Cases of Defect of Consent

Since C. 1095 is included in the chapter On Matrimonial Consent, it is clear that the phrase "cases of defect of consent" includes all three defects mentioned in that canon, namely lack of due reason, lack of due discretion and lack of due competence.

2. Due to Mental Illness

When that defect of consent is caused by a mental disorder (propter mentis morbum) then the law wants the court, as a general rule, to use the services of an expert. When, therefore, the judge has reason to believe that a mental disorder (i.e. one of the disorders included in the Diagnostic and Statistical Manual of the

American Psychiatric Association) impaired the ability of one of the parties to give marital consent, then the judge should ordinarily call upon the services of an expert.

3. *Useless*

The law explicitly excuses the judge from calling an expert when "it is obvious from the circumstances that this would be *useless*," which, in practice, can usually be translated "*superfluous*". There is an old rule of law that says, "*Eum qui certus est certiorari ulterius non oportet.*" A person who is already certain does not have to be made more certain. Many years ago the Rota applied this axiom to the question of whether the opinion of an expert was necessary in a particularly easy case. The case concerned a marriage that had taken place in China in 1916 between Peter Han, a Catholic, and Li-Koei-niu, a sixteen-year-old girl who was not a Christian. The marriage had been declared null in a Catholic tribunal in China without the use of an expert, and it came to the Rota on appeal where a confirming decision, dated June 29, 1923, was written by Monsignor Joseph Florczak. Monsignor Florczak had no problem at all with the fact that an expert had not been called in the lower court, and he commented that "although a professional report might have helped to determine the cause and nature of the mental illness, it was nevertheless not absolutely necessary since, in the case at hand, common signs of insanity were evident which would enable anyone with common sense to recognize the presence of a severe mental disorder." (15, 134). The omission of an expert's report when judged superfluous has, therefore, long been recognized as a legitimate procedure.

There is, of course, some room for interpretation here. In a given case the intervention of an expert might be regarded as superfluous by one court but not by another. Most tribunals would agree that an expert need not be called when gross lack of due discretion is patent and obvious, or when there is already ample evidence of a severe psychosexual factor like homosexuality that proved destructive of the marriage, or when the court is already in possession of medical records indicating a severe emotional disorder. But there are also grey cases in which some courts would be more reluctant than others to decide that the observations of an expert would be superfluous to the judgment about the validity of the marriage.

4. *Impossible*

Some years ago a survey of U.S. Tribunals was conducted by the author regarding their use of experts. Several of the dioceses who responded to that survey, especially those covering vast areas, noted that, for one reason or another, experts were simply not available to them. Some dioceses are too poor, and minister to people who are too poor, to be able to offer a reasonable fee for the professional services rendered. In other dioceses, where Catholics are in the minority, the tribunal is dealing perhaps most of the time with a former marriage between two non-Catholics (one of whom now wishes to marry a Catholic). Oftentimes these people are ill disposed to the Catholic Church and they are unwilling to cooperate in what they see as a kind of full-scaled investigation of their past lives. Or perhaps the area is so sparsely populated that mental health professionals are in short supply, and the tribunal is unable to locate one that has both the time and the inclination to work with the court.

In these dioceses the general sentiment is that the tribunal cannot just close its doors to its people simply because experts are not available. People want and have a right to expect a decision from their Church regarding their marital status and their freedom to remarry in the Church, and, one way or another, the Church must provide that decision. When possible, the Church's procedural law should be carefully followed in arriving at that judgment. But when the inability to adhere to a procedural law totally immobilizes a tribunal, then the law must be disregarded for the sake of the greater justice. *Ad impossibile nemo tenetur.* No one is held to the impossible.

In a December 23, 1941 decision of the Roman Rota, Monsignor Alberto Canestri applied this general principle to precisely this situation in which the local court was asked to make a decision in a matter that would ordinarily call for an expert but in which, in fact, an expert was not available. The case involved a marriage that had taken place in Tanganyika in 1931. The diocesan court had declared the marriage null without using an expert strictly so called. That decision was then appealed to the Rota where Monsignor Canestri confirmed the affirmative decision and observed that the entire procedure of the African court was, under the circumstances, "conducted with praiseworthy prudence and diligence." (33, 957).

In lieu of a professional opinion, many courts note that they are able to conclude to the marital incompetence or incapacity of a couple on the basis of the civil law criterion of "the common estimation of the ordinary man," an approach that was popularized in our circles some years ago by the decision of a certain mountain state tribunal in the case of Pamela vs. Bryan as published in *Matrimonial Jurisprudence, United States, 1968-1971.* Coupled with this approach is the conviction of many judges that, in fact, they bring to these decisions a prudence that might even exceed that of the "ordinary man," a prudence, namely, that comes from the clinical experience of working with hundreds of similar cases, plus a general background of counseling and private study. Armed thus, judges do not therefore feel altogether helpless when they are deprived of the professional advice of experts.

D. Probative Force

C. 1579 §1 says that the judge is to weigh attentively not only the conclusions of the experts but also the other circumstances of the case. This is a reminder that the judge is the *peritus peritorum* and that, besides the report of the expert, the judge must also be concerned with such questions as whether the data on which the conclusions of the expert are based are truly proved by the evidence. It is in this sense that the *dicta peritorum cribanda sunt,* i.e., that the report of the expert should be "sifted." At the same time, however, *peritis in arte credendum est* and, as Parisella noted, "When it comes to evaluating the weight and importance of the expert's report, the Rota has many times (see the decisions of 10/21/59 coram Lamas, of 8/5/54 coram Pinna, of 11/6/56 coram Mattioli, of 2/26/52 and 4/6/54 coram Felici) taught that it is wrong for the judge to depart from the conclusions of the experts except for very weighty contrary arguments." (60, 564-565).

E. Private Experts

C. 1581 notes that the parties in a case may designate their own private experts. This is a new institute in canon law; prior to the 1983 Code only the official court expert was permitted in marriage cases.

The new institute has, it seems, been little utilized in U.S. tribunals.

F. Use Of Experts

The survey mentioned above showed that, in 1978, 70 percent of the marriage cases heard by the dioceses which responded were heard on psychological grounds; the services of an expert were utilized in 56 percent of those cases.

not all are disorders

LDA

PUBLICATION

A. The Pertinent Canon

C. 1598 — §1. After the proofs have been collected the judge by a decree must, under pain of nullity, permit the parties and their advocates to inspect at the tribunal chancery the acts which are not yet known to them; a copy of the acts can also be given to advocates upon request; however, in cases concerned with the public good, in order to avoid very serious dangers, the judge can decree that a given act is not to be shown to anyone, with due concern, however, that the right of defense always remains intact.

§2. In order to complete the proofs the parties may propose additional proofs to the judge; when these have been collected there is an occasion for repeating the decree mentioned in §1 if the judge thinks it necessary.

B. The Delicacy Of Publication

1. The publication of the acts has always been viewed by the law as an extremely sensitive stage of the proceedings, precisely because of the tension that exists between the right of the two parties to know what others have said and the right of those others to have their remarks protected by confidentiality.

   A delicate balance must always be maintained between these two sets of rights, but in order to do so, different adjustments must be made in different types of cases. In *penal* cases, in which some crime is being imputed, naturally the defendant's right to know should be emphasized, whereas in a *marriage* case, in which the only issue is the bond of marriage and never the *fault or blame* of a party, then perhaps the confidentiality rights should be emphasized.

2. Recognizing confidentiality rights in marriage cases has special application, at least in the United States, both to experts and to witnesses.

   a. Were the reports of *experts* published, i.e., made available to the parties, it would not only be regarded as professionally unethical but would also subject the psychiatrist or other expert to being sued in civil court. In the case of experts, therefore, were confidentiality not recognized in chuch law, experts would have no choice but to discontinue all affiliation with ecclesiastical tribunals.

   b. As regards *witnesses,* it should be noted that some American civil lawyers are of the opinion that, at least in some states of the Union, the citizens enjoy, as a basic civil right protected by civil law, the right to convey certain information to a priest with the understanding that the information will be kept confidential. This right would include information contained in an affidavit (or in testimony) given to a priest for use in a church trial. Such information would be regarded as a privileged communication. Should the church, therefore, attempt to deprive a citizen of that civil right by ordering the judge to publicize that information which the citizen had given (and had a civil right to give) in confidence, then the offended citizen could sue the ecclesiastical judge in a civil court and impose an injunction on him requiring him to honor the confidentiality privilege of the citizen. Even apart from this possible conflict with civil law, however, the fact is that many potential witnesses in marriage cases would either decline to testify altogether or, in giving testimony, would be inhibited from total frankness if they were not assured that their remarks would be kept confidential.

C. Twentieth Century Practice Before The 1983 Code

Generally speaking the Church has, during this century (before the 1917 Code, in the 1917 Code, and in the Instruction, *Provida mater*), followed procedures that were sufficiently nuanced so as to permit the balance of rights—the balance, that is, between the right to know and the right to confidentiality.

1. *Prior to the 1917 Code*

Prior to the 1917 Code the practice in non-criminal cases was for the acts to be published only if the parties requested it, and even then the judge could decline to publish for a legitimate reason, like, for example, maintaining confidentiality. It was understood that publication was not required for validity and did not pertain to the substance of the judgment. From the point of view of the court, the purpose of publication was to establish the credibility of the parties and thereby to assure the judge that he was basing his judgment on solid information. From that point of view of the party, the purpose in petitioning a publication would be to exercise a proper defense.

2. *The 1917 Code*

The 1917 Code required that the acts be published (C. 1858) and the authors generally agreed that publication of the acts did pertain to the substance of the case, providing one of the parties requested it, with the purpose again being the right of defense. At the same time, however, the 1917 Code recognized that at least in non-consummation cases, if not all marriage cases, a publication was not necessary (C. 1985).

3. *Provida Mater*

The Instruction, *Provida Mater*, of 1936, recognizing that marriage cases involved special considerations, explicitly permitted witnesses to testify with the understanding that their names would never be revealed to the parties (Art. 130, §2). In such cases the judge was to assure himself of the credibility of the parties by obtaining testimonials, but it was, of course, permitted for the testimonials to go unpublished as well (Art. 138, §2). This procedure has been discontinued in the 1983 Code.

D. The Present Practice

1. The Balance of Rights

C. 1598 of the 1983 Code expresses rather successfully (much more so than either the 1976 draft [C. 257] or the 1980 draft [C. 1550]) the balance of rights in question. Paragraph one of the canon is in two parts. The first part states the general rule that the judge should permit the parties to inspect the acts and the advocates to be given a copy of them. The second part states an exception to the general rule, noting that in marriage cases (actually in all cases involving the public good), the judge can, under certain circumstances, declare certain acts to be completely confidential.

2. A Given Act

The phrase "aliquod actum," i.e., "a given act," suggests that, when the judge makes an exception to the general rule, a decision should be made on each individual act to be excepted. At the same time, however, it is clear that a judge may, as a general policy, decide to exclude certain categories of evidence, e.g., the reports of experts, from publication.

3. Very Serious Dangers

The canon notes that a judge may except certain acts from publication "ad gravissima pericula evitanda"—in order to avoid very serious dangers. In attempting to determine more specifically what those dangers might be, one might look to C. 1455 §3 which permits a judge to bind all parties to secrecy for the following reasons: to avoid dissension, scandal, or the endangerment of a person's reputation. See also C. 1548 §2, 2°.

4. The Right of Defense

The canon notes that, even when a party's right to know is restricted, the "right of defense" must "always" remain intact. Two things are noteworthy here: first, the right of defense, which has historically always been regarded as one of the essential reasons for publication, is now mentioned explicitly in the canon; secondly, the canon recognizes that, at least in certain cases, the right of defense and the right of the parties to know are separable rights—the first can be observed without the second. This is particularly true in a marriage case in which the issue is not the good name of either party but the validity of the marriage bond. From the time of Benedict XIV, and more specifically from the promulgation in 1741 of his *Dei miseratione*, in which the "defensor matrimonii" was called for in every diocese, it has been understood that, in a marriage case, the "ius defensionis" belongs principally and primarily not to the respondent but to the defender of the bond. This point was made explicitly in a rotal decision of November 27, 1958 coram Brennan. The Code does well, therefore, to recognize that under certain conditions, some acts may be withheld from the parties but must, nevertheless, be shown to the defender (the tenor and extent of this canon would not seem to include the defender when it says that the judge may decide that a certain act not be shown to "anyone"—"nemini") so that the right of defense remains intact.

For more on the Right of Defense, see pages 72-73

5. *Names of the Witnesses*

Even in those cases in which the judge decides to withhold certain evidence from publication, the parties have a right to know the names of all the witnesses, though not those of the affiants.

6. *The Absent Respondent*

When a party has been declared absent in accord with C. 1592, he or she need not be afforded the right to inspect the acts at this time.

For more on the absent respondent see page 29.

7. *The Decree of Publication, etc.*

When all the evidence seems to be in, the judge issues the Decree of Publication. Since, however, most of the evidence has, by that time, been classified as confidential, the Decree (most tribunals use a standard form) turns out, in practice, to be more a Decree of Confidentiality than a Decree of Publication.

At any rate, following that decree, the judge then issues the Decree of Closing, the closing, namely, of the evidence gathering stage of the trial (C. 1599).

Once that stage has closed then the discussion phase of the trial begins. During this stage the advocate and defender write their briefs and animadversions (pages 21-22 and 25-26) following which, unless the petitioner renounces the instance, the judge pronounces the sentence.

RENUNCIATION

A. The Pertinent Canons

C. 1524 — §1. A petitioner can renounce the instance at any stage or grade of trial; both petitioner and respondent can likewise renounce either all or some of the acts of the process.

§2. In order for them to renounce an instance, the guardians and administrators of juridic persons need to consult with or obtain the consent of those whose involvement is required to place acts which go beyond the limits of ordinary administration.

§3. In order for a renunciation to be valid it is to be made in writing and also signed by the party or by the party's procurator with a special mandate to do so; it must be communicated to the other party, accepted, or at least not attacked, by that party, and admitted by the judge.

C. 1525 — A renunciation admitted by the judge has the same effects concerning the renounced acts as an abatement of an instance and it obliges the renouncing party to pay the expenses for the renounced acts.

B. Definition

The renunciation of an instance is a declaration by the petitioner that he or she wishes to terminate the process prior to the sentence.

C. Utility

Renunciation is widely used in American tribunals as a way of avoiding a formal negative sentence.

A marriage is not regarded as definitively null until there have been two conforming affirmative sentences. Once, therefore, a court of first instance gives a formal negative sentence in a case, then the petitioner in that case must, in order to be regarded as free to marry, bring the case to two more courts, which will usually be the ordinary court of appeals (for second instance) and the Roman Rota (for third instance). Because of the time and the expenses involved plus the strain of living with uncertainty for such an extended period of time, most people are extremely reluctant to go to the Rota. If, therefore, it appears, during the first instance proceeding, that there is not enough evidence to warrant an affirmative decision at that time, most petitioners prefer to renounce the instance prior to the sentence and thus bring the proceeding to a temporary closure in the hope that future developments, either in the availability of proofs or in the jurisprudence of the court, will improve their chances for an affirmative decision at a later date.

Once the instance has been renounced by the petitioner, the tribunal then usually lists the case, for statistical purposes, as having received a "non-affirmative" or "informal negative" decision. The CLSA *1985 Proceedings* show that, in 1984, the first instance tribunals of the United States gave 3128 such decisions.

D. Conditions

In order for a renunciation to be valid, three conditions must be fulfilled. These three conditions refer to the petitioner, the respondent and the judge.

1. *The Petitioner*

The renunciation should be in writing and signed by the petitioner (or by the petitioner's proxy with a special mandate of renunciation).

This may be done either at the time of the petition and included as an appendage to the petition or at the point where the tribunal informs the petitioner that the available evidence, in the judgment of the court, does not warrant an affirmative decision. If the *former*, the renunciation is made conditionally ("should the court, just prior to sentencing, not be able to reach an affirmative decision in my case" etc.). If the *latter*, a typical statement of renunciation might read as follows:

Woodcock-Widgeon

To the Tribunal of _____

In accord with C. 1524 I hereby withdraw my petition in the above named case with the understanding that I am free to reopen these proceedings whenever I wish.

Signature _____

It should be noted, finally, that when it is clear that the petitioner *intends* to renounce the instance but through ignorance or negligence either on the part of the petitioner or on the part of the procurator, a valid renunciation is not in fact lodged, then the judge, in order to avoid an unjust sentence, should, in accord with C. 1452 §2, arrange ex officio for a valid renunciation.

2. *The Respondent*

The renunciation should be communicated to the respondent and, as a general rule, be accepted or at least not attacked by the respondent.

Unless the respondent is personally interested in obtaining a church annulment, the respondent does not usually offer any objections to the case being withdrawn. The letter of notification to the respondent might read as follows:

Dear Mr. Widgeon

Some months ago, as you know, Elizabeth asked this court for a declaration of nullity in respect to her marriage to you. Now, however, Elizabeth has decided not to pursue the matter after all. Unless you have some feeling to the contrary, therefore, we shall regard the case as officially withdrawn.

Sincerely yours,

In those cases where the respondent *does* object to a renunciation, the judge, contrary to the general rule stated in C. 1524 §3, is still free, after hearing the Defender of the Bond, to admit the renunciation anyway. This was specifically permitted for the Rota by article 89 §2 of the 1934 Norms for the Rota (AAS 26, p. 472) and, based on this rotal practice, was regarded by the authors as a legitimate procedure in other courts as well. It is, however, an exception and should be utilized only when circumstances warrant it.

3. *The Judge*

A renunciation must be admitted by the judge prior to the sentence.

C. 1524 §1 states that the petitioner may renounce the instance at any stage of the trial. Since, however, C. 1517 states that an instance ends with the pronounce-ment of the definitive sentence, then clearly a renunciation may be made and admitted by the judge at any time up to the pronouncement of the sentence but not after that time.

In the event that the case were being heard by a collegiate tribunal this would mean that a renunciation could be admitted certainly after the discussion among the three judges mentioned in C. 1609 °3 and probably even after the sentence itself had been signed by the judges (since, according to C. 1614 the sentence has no force prior to publication) but definitely not after the publication of the sentence.

E. Effects

The effects of renunciation are basically two:

1. A renunciation extinguishes the acts of the *process* (i.e. it ends the instance) but not the acts of the *case* (i.e. the evidence may be used later, even in another competent court [*AAS* 78, p. 1324] should the case be revived).

2. A renunciation obliges the petitioner to pay a reasonable fee for the proceedings conducted up to that time.

SENTENCE

A. The Pertinent Canons

C. 1608 — §1. For the pronouncement of any kind of sentence, there must be in the mind of the judge moral certitude regarding the matter to be settled by the sentence.

§2. The judge must derive this certitude from the acts and the proofs.

§3. However, the judge must evaluate the proofs conscientiously with due regard for the prescriptions of the law concerning the efficacy of certain proofs.

§4. A judge who cannot arrive at this certitude, is to pronounce that the right of the petitioner is not established, and is to dismiss the respondent as absolved, unless there is question of a case which enjoys the favor of the law, in which case the decision must be in favor of it.

C. 1609 — §1. If the tribunal is collegiate, the presiding judge of the college is to determine on what day and at what hour the judges are to convene for their deliberation; and the meeting is to be held at the tribunal unless a special reason suggests otherwise.

§2. On the day assigned for the meeting, the judges shall individually submit in writing their conclusions on the merits of the case and the reasons, both in law and in fact, for arriving at these conclusions, which are to be appended to the acts of the case and are to be kept secret.

§3. After the invocation of the Divine Name, the conclusions of the individual judge are to be made known in the order of precedence, but beginning always with the *ponens* or the *relator* of the case, and there is to be a discussion under the leadership of the presiding judge, especially in order to decide what is to be determined in the dispositive part of the sentence.

§4. In discussion, however, each judge has the right to retract his or her original conclusions; on the other hand, a judge who does not wish to accede to the decision of the others, can demand that his or her conclusions be transmitted to the higher tribunal if there is an appeal.

§5. But if the judges are unwilling or unable to arrive at a sentence in the first discussion, the decision can be deferred to another meeting but not beyond one week unless the instruction of the case must be completed in accord with the norm of C. 1600.

C. 1610 — §1. If there is only one judge, he himself will write the sentence.

§ 2. In a collegiate tribunal it is the duty of the *ponens* or *relator* to write the

66

sentence, drawing the reasons from those which the individual judges brought out in the discussion, unless it has been previously decided by the majority of the judges which reasons are to be preferred; then the sentence is to be submitted for the approval of the individual judges.

§3. The sentence must be issued not beyond one month from the day on which the case was settled, unless, in a collegiate tribunal, the judges set a longer period of time for a serious reason.

C. 1611 — A sentence must:

1° settle the controversy discussed before the tribunal with an appropriate response given to each one of the questions;

2° determine what obligations of the parties arise from the trial and how they must be fulfilled;

3° set forth the reasons, that is, the motives both in law and in fact on which the dispositive section of the sentence is based;

4° make a determination about the expenses of the suit.

C. 1612 — §1. After the invocation of the Divine Name, the sentence must express in sequence who is the judge or the tribunal; who is the petitioner, the respondent, the procurator, with the names and domiciles correctly indicated; the promoter of justice and the defender of the bond, if they took part in the trial.

§2. Next, it must briefly report the facts together with the conclusions of the parties and the formulation of the doubts.

§3. Following these points is the dispositive section of the sentence preceded by the reasons on which it is based.

§4. It is to close with an indication of the day and place where it was rendered and with the signature of the judge or, if it is a collegiate tribunal, with the signatures of all the judges and the notary.

C. 1613 — The regulations mentioned above concerning a definitive sentence are to be adapted to an interlocutory sentence.

C. 1614 — The sentence is to be published as soon as possible with an indication of the ways in which it can be challenged; it has no force before publication even if the dispositive section has been made known to the parties with the permission of the judge.

C. 1615 — The publication or announcement of the sentence can be made either by giving a copy of the sentence to the parties or their procurators or by sending a copy to them in accord with the norm of C. 1509.

C. 1616 — §1. If in the text of the sentence either an error in calculations has crept in, or a material error has occurred in transcribing the dispositive section, or reporting the facts or the petitions of the parties, or if the points required by C. 1612 §4 were omitted, the sentence must be corrected or completed at the request of the parties or ex officio by the tribunal which issued the sentence; the parties, moreover, must always be heard and a decree appended at the bottom of the sentence.

§2. If any party objects, the incidental question is to be settled by decree.

B. Definition

A definitive sentence is a legitimate pronouncement by which a judge settles a principal case that was proposed by litigants and was tried judicially.

C. Moral Certitude

Pius XII, in his allocution to the Rota on October 1, 1942, noted that moral certainty exists between the two extremes of absolute certainty on the one hand and quasi-certainty or probability on the other. It is, he said

> characterized on the positive side by the exclusion of well-founded or reasonable doubt, and in this respect it is essentially distinguished from the quasi-certainty which has been mentioned; on the negative side, it does admit the absolute possibility of the contrary, and in this it differs from absolute certainty. The certainty of which We are now speaking is necessary and sufficient for the rendering of a judgment, even though in the particular case it would be possible either directly or indirectly to reach absolute certainty. Only thus is it possible to have a regular and orderly administration of justice, going forward without useless delays and without laying excessive burdens on the tribunal as well as on the parties.

For a copy of the entire allocution see Appendix Five on page 121.

D. Some Observations

The canons on the sentence speak for themselves and need little commentary. Perhaps, however, the following points deserve mention:

1. *Sample Sentences*

The book *Decisions,* published by the Canon Law Society of America contains an outline of a sentence plus thirty-nine sample sentences on various grounds of nullity.

2. The Parts of a Sentence

C. 1609 §3, among others, speaks of the "dispositive" part of a sentence. The *dispositive* part of a sentence refers to the actual decision or judgment (affirmative or negative) and is usually stated in a sentence or two. The rest of the sentence (the facts, the law and the argument) are known as the *expositive* part of the sentence.

3. The Ponens

C. 1609 §3 and C. 1610 §2 speak of the "ponens." The ponens is sometimes called the "commissioner" since it is the ponens or relator who commits the final sentence to writing.

In the event that the person originally appointed as ponens is, at the time of the decision, outvoted by the other two judges, the usual procedure is to appoint, in accord with C. 1429, one of the majority judges as substitute commissioner for the drafting of the sentence. In lieu of that procedure, the outvoted judge-ponens should carefully draw, as recommended in C. 1610 §2, on the reasons of the other two judges in support of the final decision of the college.

4. The Publication of the Sentence

C. 1614 and C. 1615 speak of the publication of the sentence. The publication of the sentence should not be seen as entirely divorced from the publication of the acts (C. 1598). If, for example, the judge withheld certain acts from being published, and classified them as secret in order to avoid serious dangers, then that evidence should still be considered secret at the time of the publication of the sentence. This could, therefore, involve either deleting certain passages from the sentence for publication purposes, even if published to a procurator, or perhaps even publishing only the dispositive part of the sentence.

When a court of first instance publishes an affirmative decision to the respondent, the letter of publication customarily informs the respondent that the case will automatically go on appeal to the court of second instance. In accord with C. 1614, the respondent should also, in some way, be apprised of his or her right to a personal appeal; this is generally done, however, in a way that does not promote or encourage unnecessary appeals by respondents.

COMPLAINT OF NULLITY

A. The Pertinent Canons

C. 1620 — A sentence is vitiated by irremediable nullity if:

1° it was rendered by a judge who is absolutely incompetent;

2° it was rendered by a person who lacks the power of judging in the tribunal in which the case was settled;

3° the judge passed the sentence under duress from force or grave fear;

4° the trial was instituted without the judicial petition mentioned in C. 1501, or was not instituted against some respondent;

5° it was rendered between parties one of whom at least did not have standing in court;

6° one person acted in the name of another without a legitimate mandate;

7° the right of defense was denied to one or other party;

8° it did not settle the controversy even partially.

C. 1621 — The complaint of nullity mentioned in C. 1620 can always be proposed by way of exception in perpetuity and by way of action before the judge who pronounced the sentence within ten years from the date of publication of the sentence.

C. 1622 — A sentence is vitiated by remediable nullity only, if:

1° it was rendered by an illegitimate number of judges contrary to the prescription of C. 1425 §1;

2° it does not contain the motives, that is, the reasons for the decision;

3° it lacks the signatures prescribed by law;

4° it does not contain reference to the year, month, day and place in which it was pronounced;

5° it is based on a judicial act which is null and whose nullity was not sanated according to the norm of C. 1619;

6° it was rendered against a party who was legitimately absent as provided for in C. 1593 §2.

C. 1623 — The complaint of nullity in the cases mentioned in C. 1622 can be proposed within three months from the notification of publication of the sentence.

C. 1624 — The judge who pronounced the sentence examines the complaint of nullity; but if the party fears that the judge who pronounced the sentence which is being challenged by the complaint of nullity, may be prejudiced and, as a result, regards him or her as suspect, the party can demand that another judge be substituted according to the norm of C. 1450.

C. 1625 — A complaint of nullity can be proposed together with an appeal within the time determined for an appeal.

C. 1626 — §1. Not only the parties who feel themselves aggrieved can file a complaint of nullity but also the promoter of justice or the defender of the bond whenever they have the right to intervene.

§2. A judge himself can ex officio retract or amend an invalid sentence which he has pronounced, within the time period for acting set by C. 1623 unless meanwhile an appeal together with a complaint of nullity has been filed, or unless the nullity has been sanated during the course of the time mentioned in C. 1623.

C. 1627 — Cases involving a complaint of nullity can be treated according to the norms for the oral contentious process.

B. Definition

A complaint of nullity (querela nullitatis) is the impugning of a judicial sentence by which one claims that the sentence suffers from some substantial defect and is therefore null.

C. Division

The complaint can claim either remediable (curable) or irremediable (incurable) nullity. The distinction is based on the purely practical question of whether it can or cannot be healed. *Remediable* nullity is automatically healed after three months if no complaint is lodged against it (C. 1623 with C. 1465 §1). It can also be healed, generally speaking, simply by correcting the error of omission that caused the nullity. *Irremediable* nullity, on the other hand, is open to perpetual challenge and can never really be healed. On the contrary, for the trial to be valid, it must be repeated in its entirety.

D. The Right Of Defense

Generally the canons on complaint of nullity of sentence are self explanatory.
Number seven of C. 1620, however, which states that a sentence is vitiated by
irremediable nullity if the right of defense was denied to one or the other, deserves
some comment.

1. *When the sentence is NEGATIVE*

When the sentence is negative there could be a claim that the *petitioner's* right of
defense was denied. This would be justified when a petitioner was not advised of
his or her right to appoint an advocate and was thus deprived of counsel. Perhaps
the mere lack of an advocate's services would not automatically amount to a
denial of the right of defense in every case, since some cases would clearly be
unsalvageable even with the best of advocates. When, however, it can be shown
1) that the petitioner was not apprised of his or her right to an advocate and 2) that
the services of an advocate would probably have resulted either in generating
additional evidence or in presenting to the court a reasonably convincing
argument in favor of nullity, then it would appear that a complaint of nullity would
be justified.

2. *When the sentence is AFFIRMATIVE*

When the sentence is affirmative, there could be a claim that the *defender's* right
of defense was denied. The principal issue in a marriage case is not a party's virtue
or lack thereof; the principal issue in every marriage case is the bond. Therefore,
only when the defender of the bond has been deprived of his or her right to
defend the bond has the "right of defense" been denied. It cannot be said that the
right of defense has been denied if, for example, the respondent is not allowed to
see every document in its entirety (C. 1598 §1). In a rotal decision coram Brennan
of November 27, 1958, it was made clear 1) that "in a contentious case properly
so called," the petitioner and respondent must indeed be given the total right of
defending themselves — otherwise the entire process would be null by reason of
the natural law in that an element that would be essentially constitutive of a trial
would be lacking, but 2) that in a marriage case the right of defense is sufficiently
honored if the defender of the bond is afforded the right. This is not to say, of
course, that the parties need not be cited or that the acts need not be published,
but only that essentially the right of defense is protected in a marriage case as long
as the defender is afforded the right.

C. 1622, 6° also seems to favor this position. The Code, by including this canon as
separate from C. 1620, 7°, seems to take the position that the right of defense is not
necessarily denied simply because the respondent never received any notices
from the court after the original citation. To put it another way, an absent

respondent who, after the sentence, demonstrates that his or her absenteeism was inculpable, then has an automatic right to lodge a complaint of *curable* nullity by reason of C. 1622, 6°; he or she does not necessarily, however, have the automatic right to claim incurable nullity by reason of C. 1620, 7°. If he or she did, C. 1622, 6° would be superfluous.

As regards the Right of Defense as it bears on publication of the acts, see pages 61-62.

APPEAL

A. The Pertinent Canons

C. 1628 — The party who feels aggrieved by a given sentence and likewise the promoter of justice and the defender of the bond in cases in which their presence is required, have the right to appeal from a sentence to a higher judge, with due regard for the prescription of C. 1629.

C. 1629 — There is no room for appeal:

   1° from a sentence of the Supreme Pontiff himself or of the Apostolic Signatura;

   2° from a sentence vitiated by nullity unless it is joined with a complaint of nullity according to the norm of C. 1625;

   3° from a sentence which has become *res iudicata;*

   4° from a decree of a judge or an interlocutory sentence which does not have the force of a definitive sentence, unless it is joined with an appeal from a definitive sentence;

   5° from a sentence or from a decree in a case in which the law provides for a settlement of the matter as quickly as possible.

C. 1630 — §1. An appeal must be filed before the judge who pronounced the sentence within the peremptory time limit of fifteen available days (*tempus utile*) from notification of the publication of the sentence.

§2. If it is made orally, the notary is to put it in writing in the presence of the appellant.

C. 1631 — If a question arises regarding the right of appeal, the appellate tribunal should examine it as quickly as possible according to the norms of the oral contentious process.

C. 1632 — §1. If in the appeal there is no indication of the tribunal to which it is directed, it is presumed to be made to the tribunal mentioned in C. 1438 and C. 1439.

§2. If the other party has recourse to another appellate tribunal, the tribunal of higher grade examines the case, with due regard for C. 1415.

C. 1633 — An appeal must be prosecuted within a month of its being filed before the judge to whom it is directed, unless the judge from whom appeal is made has set a longer period of time for the party to prosecute it.

C. 1634 — §1. In order to prosecute an appeal, it is required and suffices that the party call upon the services of the higher judge for the emendation of the challenged sentence, append a copy of this sentence, and indicate the reasons for the appeal.

§2. If the party is unable to obtain a copy of the challenged sentence from the tribunal from which the appeal is being made within the available time, the time limits do not run out in the interval; and the impediment must be indicated to the appellate judge who is to bind the judge from whom the appeal is made with a precept to perform his duty as soon as possible.

§3. Meanwhile the judge from whom the appeal is being made must transmit the acts to the appellate judge according to the norm of C. 1474.

C. 1635 — If the deadline for appeal either before the judge from whom the appeal is being made or before the judge to whom the appeal is directed has passed without result, the appeal is considered abandoned.

C. 1636 — §1. The appellant can renounce the appeal with the effects mentioned in C. 1525.

§2. If the appeal was proposed by the defender of the bond or the promoter of justice, it can be renounced by the defender of the bond or the promoter of justice of the appellate tribunal unless the law provides otherwise.

C. 1637 — §1. An appeal lodged by the petitioner also benefits the respondent and vice versa.

§2. If there are several respondents or petitioners, and if the sentence is challenged by only one or against only one of them, the challenge is considered made by all of them and against all of them whenever the matter sought is indivisible or it is a joint obligation.

§3. If an appeal is filed by one party regarding one part of the sentence, the other party can place an incidental appeal regarding the other parts within a peremptory time period of fifteen days from the date of being notified of the principal appeal even though the deadline for an appeal has expired.

§4. Unless there is evidence to the contrary, it is presumed that an appeal is made against all parts of the sentence.

C. 1638 — An appeal suspends the execution of a sentence.

C. 1682 — §1. The sentence which first declared the nullity of the marriage together with the appeals if there are any and the other acts of the trial, are to be sent ex officio to the appellate tribunal within twenty days from the publication of the sentence.

B. Definition

An appeal is a recourse to a higher court against a sentence given by a lower court.

This definition rightly implies that an appeal may be lodged against either a first instance or a second instance decision. In a marriage case, however, a simple appeal is permitted against a second instance decision only when it has *reversed* the decision of the first instance court. When the appellate court *confirms* the decision of the first instance court, i.e. when there are two concordant sentences, then a simple appeal is not permitted but only the New Presentation *(Nova Propositio)* mentioned in C. 1644. Since, however, the New Presentation occurs only after the sentence of an appellate court, it is treated in the chapter after next on appellate procedures. See page 82.

C. The Appellant

A sentence may be appealed either by the parties, the defender or the legislator.

1. The Parties

As alluded to in the chapter on Renunciation, the formal negative sentence is rare in American tribunals; generally the negative sentence is avoided by the petitioner's renouncing of the instance prior to the actual sentence. In those cases in which a negative sentence is given, however, the *petitioner* will usually appeal.

Contrariwise, although the *respondent* enjoys the right to appeal against an affirmative decision, the experience of the first few years following the 1983 Code has shown that only about two percent of respondents have actually exercised that right.

As regards the right of the absent respondent to appeal, see page 29.

2. The Defender of the Bond

The Defender of the Bond, like the respondent, enjoys the right to appeal against an affirmative decision. In practice, however, defenders seem to exercise that right only when they are personally convinced in their own minds that the decision of the court is erroneous, that in fact the nullity of the marriage has not been proved. The Code itself does not provide defenders with any guidelines on when it might be appropriate for them to appeal but personal conviction about the incorrectness of an affirmative decision would seem to be a suitable rule of thumb.

3. The Legislator

The legislator or the law, specifically C. 1682 §1, is certainly the principal appellant in all marriage cases which receive an affirmative decision in first instance. That canon directs that even if neither the respondent nor the defender appeals an affirmative decision, the case must nevertheless be sent to the appellate court and be reviewed at that level. In practice more than ninety-five percent of all first instance affirmatives are sent to the court of appeals only by reason of C. 1682 §1.

D. The Court Of Second Instance

The court of second instance can be either the *ordinary* court of appeals in the United States or the *extraordinary* court of appeals, namely the Roman Rota.

1. The Ordinary Court

Ordinarily the court of second instance will, depending on the local arrangement, be either the metropolitan court (C. 1438, 1°), the designated (arch)diocesan court (C. 1438, 2°) or the interdiocesan court (C. 1439 §2).

C. 1632 §1 notes that unless an appeal is specifically directed to the Rota, it is presumed to be made to the ordinary court of appeals; and C. 1682 §1 indicates that all affirmative decisions appealed "by the legislator" are sent to that same court, namely the ordinary appellate court.

2. The Extraordinary Court

C. 1444 §1, 1° indicates that the parties have the right to bypass the ordinary appellate court and appeal a first instance decision directly to the Rota. Occasionally a respondent, feeling that all American tribunals are too liberal and that the only fair hearing is available in Rome, will insist that eventually he or she plans to appeal to Rome itself. These people should be advised that, if a Roman hearing is an absolute priority with them, they should consider appealing the *first* instance affirmative decision to Rome because if the case were heard in second instance by the ordinary appellate court and if that court were to issue a second affirmative decision, then, unless the respondent could bring forward "new and serious proofs or arguments" which were not adduced in the first two instances, then the respondent would not be granted a third instance, in Rome or anywhere else (C. 1644 §1).

Having a case heard at the Rota, however, does involve considerable expense, and interested respondents should, of course, be apprised of this as well.

REINSTATEMENT

A. The Pertinent Canons

C. 1645 — §1. *Restitutio in integrum* is granted against a sentence which has become a *res judicata* provided that there is clear proof of its injustice.

§2. However, clear proof of injustice is verified only if:

1° the sentence is so based on proofs which are later discovered to be false so that without those proofs the dispositive section of the sentence would not be sustained;

2° afterwards documents have been found which undoubtedly prove new facts which demand a contrary decision;

3° the sentence was pronounced because of the fraud of one party which harmed the other;

4° a prescription of the law which is not merely procedural has been evidently neglected;

5° the sentence is contrary to a preceding sentence which has become a *res iudicata.*

C. 1646 — §1.*Restitutio in integrum* for the reasons mentioned in C.1645 §2, nn. 1-3 must be sought from the judge who issued the sentence, within three months to be computed from the date of one's becoming aware of the reasons.

§2. *Restitutio in integrum* for the reasons mentioned in C.1645 §2, nn. 4 and 5 must be sought from the appellate tribunal within three months from notification of the publication of the sentence; but if, in the case mentioned in C. 1645 §2, n. 5, notification of the preceding decision is had later, the time limit runs from this notification.

§3. The time limits mentioned above do not expire as long as the injured person is a minor.

C. 1647 — §1. A petition of *restitutio in integrum* suspends the execution of a sentence if the execution has not yet begun.

§2. If, however, from probable indications there is a suspicion that the petition has been made in order to delay the execution of the sentence, the judge can decree that the sentence be executed but with due caution being taken to indemnify the person seeking *restitutio in integrum* if it is granted.

C. 1648 — If *restitutio in integrum* is granted, the judge must pronounce on the merits of the case.

B. Definition

Reinstatement (*restitutio in integrum*) is a legal remedy by which a person who has been seriously injured by a judicial sentence that was manifestly unjust can, for reasons of natural equity, be restored by a competent judge to the status quo *ante,* i.e., before the injurious sentence.

C. Reinstatement In A First Instance Decision

1. C. 1645 §1 says that reinstatement may be used ("datur") against a *res iudicata.*

2. A *res iudicata* or closed judgment is a definitive judicial sentence which is so firm and final that it no longer admits either of appeal or of complaint of nullity but only of reinstatement.

3. Reinstatement, in other words, is the *only* remedy against a closed judgment. It seems, however, that reinstatement need not be *restricted* to closed judgments, but may apply to other judgments as well, even to a first instance decision in a marriage case, providing, of course, that the sentence was "manifestly unjust" for one of the reasons stated in c. 1645 §2.

D. Some Examples

1. A court of first instance gives an affirmative decision in a case in which the allegation was that the petitioner simulated marriage by an intention *contra bonum sacramenti.* The decision was reached largely on the basis of the testimony of the best man who told the court, in great detail, of a conversation he had had with the petitioner a few weeks before the marriage in which the petitioner confessed that he did not really love his fiancée, planned a trial marriage, etc. Two weeks after the sentence was issued, however, the best man was overcome with guilt, visited with the judge and retracted his testimony, saying that he had perjured himself because the petitioner's father had paid him $500 to do so. The court of *first* instance could grant reinstatement by reason of C. 1646 §1.

2. A petitioner in a first instance proceeding, realizing that she is unable, at the present time, to gather enough evidence to prove nullity, renounces the instance in accord with C. 1524. The court, however, overlooks the renunciation and proceeds to issue a negative sentence. The court of *second* instance could then grant reinstatement on the basis of C. 1646 §2.

APPELLATE PROCEDURES

A. The Pertinent Canons

C. 1682 — §1. The sentence which first declared the nullity of the marriage together with the appeals if there are any and the other acts of the trial, are to be sent ex officio to the appellate tribunal within twenty days from the publication of the sentence.

§2. If the sentence rendered in favor of the nullity of marriage was in the first grade of trial, the appellate tribunal by its own decree is to confirm the decision without delay or admit the case to an ordinary examination of a new grade of trial, after considering the observations of the defender of the bond and those of the parties if there are any.

C. 1683 — If at the appellate level a new ground of nullity of the marriage is offered, the tribunal can admit it and judge it as if in first instance.

C. 1684 — §1. After the sentence which first declared the nullity of marriage has been confirmed at the appellate level either by decree or by another sentence, those persons whose marriage was declared null can contract new marriages immediately after the decree or the second sentence has been made known to them unless a prohibition is attached to this sentence or decree, or it is prohibited by a determination of the local ordinary.

§2. The prescriptions of C. 1644 must be observed, even if the sentence which declared the nullity of marriage was not confirmed by another sentence but by a decree.

C. 1685 — Immediately after the sentence has been executed, the judicial vicar must notify the ordinary of the place in which the marriage was celebrated about this. He must take care that notation be made quickly in the matrimonial and baptismal registers concerning the nullity of the marriage and any prohibitions which may have been determined.

C. 1644 — §1. If two concordant sentences have been pronounced in a case concerning the status of persons, it can be appealed at any time to an appellate tribunal if new and serious proofs or arguments are brought forward within the peremptory time period of thirty days from the proposed challenge. However, within a month from the presentation of the new proofs and arguments, the appellate tribunal must settle by decree whether a new presentation of the case must be admitted or not.

§2. An appeal to a higher tribunal to obtain a new presentation of the case does not suspend the execution of the sentence, unless either the law provides otherwise or the appellate tribunal orders its suspension, in accord with the norm of C. 1650 §3.

B. The Court Of Appeal

Ordinarily, as noted in the chapter on Appeal (Section D. - page 77), the court of second instance will, depending on the local arrangement, be either the metropolitan court (C. 1438, 1°), the designated (arch)diocesan court (C. 1438, 2°), or the interdiocesan court (C. 1439 §2).

C. Ratification Or New Hearing

According to C. 1682 §2, it is the collegiate tribunal (a single judge is permitted only in first instance — C. 1425 §4) which determines whether the first instance affirmative decision will simply be ratified or awarded a new hearing. Conceivably, therefore, both the respondent and the defender might appeal the first instance decision and request a new hearing but the judges might, in spite of this, decide simply to ratify. That certainly would not be the usual procedure but the point deserves to be made that it is the judges and no one else who decide whether the case will be ratified or given an ordinary examination.

D. Conformity Of Grounds

1. *Affirmative in First Instance*

Some rotal decisions (see, for example, 66, 340-341) have held that when an appellate court, using the same juridic facts as the lower court, finds in the affirmative but on a ground slightly different from that of the lower court, the two sentences may be regarded as equivalently concordant.

2. *Negative in First Instance*

This rule does not apply, however, when the decision in first instance was negative. Therefore, should the first instance court give a negative decision on, say, the grounds of the respondent's lack of due *discretion,* this would not prohibit the appellate court, using substantially the same evidence, from giving an affirmative decision on the grounds of the respondent's lack of due *competence,* and regarding it not as a reversal of the first instance decision but as a wholly new ground.

E. Adding A New Ground Of Nullity

C. 1683 notes that, if the appellate court accepts a new ground of nullity, it may judge the case on that ground "as if in *first* instance." The question then arises, however, as to where the case should be heard in *second* instance. If it is a *metropolitan* court that adds the new ground then, of course, the case goes to that metropolitan's ordinary appellate court (C. 1438, 2°). If, however, it is an *interdiocesan* court that adds the new ground, then the appeal would have to be directed to the Rota since interdiocesan appellate courts are not customarily assigned a United States court of appeals.

F. The Ratification Process

1. The tribunal first hears from the defender. That defender, as noted in the chapter devoted to that office (Section F - page 23) is usually distinct from the defender in first instance but not necessarily so.

2. The tribunal also considers the observations of the parties if there are any.

3. The college then proceeds as a collegial body (collegialiter — C. 1426 §1) to issue the decree. A sample decree of ratification may be found on page 196 of *Decisions.*

G. The Right To Remarry

According to C. 1684 §1, after the first instance sentence is confirmed at the appellate level, the parties are, unless a prohibition is attached (see the next chapter), free to enter new marriages. At that point, in other words, there is a *res quasi iudicata* or a quasi closed judgment.

H. New Presentation *(Nova Propositio)*

1. Generally speaking an appeal is not permitted after there have been two concordant sentences, either affirmative or negative.

2. By way of exception, however, an appeal is permitted if "new and serious proofs or arguments" can be brought forward. This exceptional appeal to third instance after two concordant sentences is known as a New Presentation.

3. Unlike the regular appeal, a New Presentation is, in itself, non-suspensive. If, therefore, a New Presentation was lodged after a second affirmative decision, the parties would still be free to remarry immediately. It should, however, be kept in mind, that when the New Presentation arrives at the Rota, the Rota might, in accord with c. 1644 §2, order remarriage rights suspended until further notice.

I. Norms

For a copy of the Norms issued by the Signatura in 1970 for interdiocesan courts see Appendix two on page 102.

PROHIBITION

A. The Pertinent Canons

C. 1684 — §. After the sentence which first declared the nullity of marriage has been confirmed at the appellate level either by decree or by another sentence, those persons whose marriage was declared null can contract new marriages immediately after the decree or the second sentence has been made known to them unless a prohibition is attached to this sentence or decree, or it is prohibited by a determination of the local ordinary.

f. C. 1077
Bishop delegating marriage

§2. The prescriptions of C. 1644 must be observed, even if the sentence which declared the nullity of marriage was not confirmed by another sentence but by a decree.

C. 1685 — Immediately after the sentence has been executed, the judicial vicar must notify the ordinary of the place in which the marriage was celebrated about this. He must take care that notation be made quickly in the matrimonial and baptismal registers concerning the nullity of the marriage and any prohibitions which may have been determined.

B. Definition

A prohibition (*vetitum*) is a restriction imposed either by a tribunal or by a local ordinary on a party, limiting or conditioning to some extent that party's right to remarry.

C. Practice

It is clear from the "Survey on the Use of the *Vetitum*" by Charles Guarino and William Varvaro (*CLSAP* 1983, 285-289), from "The *Vetitum* and *Monitum* in Matrimonial Nullity Proceedings" by Jack Hopka (*Studia Canonica* 1985, 357-399) and from "The Prohibition Imposed by a Tribunal: Law, Practice, Future Development" by John Lucas (*The Jurist*, 1985, 588-617) that there is great disparity among tribunals regarding the use of prohibitions. Hopka (p. 397) summarizes it this way:

> There exists a wide divergence among the tribunals of the United States in regard to three points. First, there is much variation in the actual description of the terms *vetitum* and *monitum*. Second, there is a variety of persons and groups of persons responsible for the imposition of a *vetitum* or *monitum*. Third, there exists an extreme diversity among the tribunals as to which person or persons are responsible for lifting the *vetitum* or *monitum*.

> A general consensus can be found among the tribunals of the United States in several areas. The criteria both for the imposition and lifting of *vetita* and *monita* follow generally the same lines, although with various degrees of strictness. Most tribunals will impose a *vetitum* or *monitum* on the respondent,

regardless of religious affiliation. The appellate tribunal will always uphold a *vetitum* or *monitum* imposed by a court of first instance, and will sometimes even impose one of its own. Most tribunals report "good experiences" with *monita* and *vetita,* often adding that much depends on the way these concepts are presented to the principals in the nullity case.

The most frequent use of a prohibition occurs when a party is found by a tribunal to have lacked due competence for a first marriage with strong indications that competence for a second marriage could likewise be lacking. A prohibition, however, might also be appropriate in cases where a party was found to be impotent or to have simulated or where a party shows signs of having permanently impaired discretionary powers.

D. Force

In accord with C. 1077 §2, it is clear that all prohibitions imposed by diocesan, metropolitan or interdiocesan courts affect only the liceity and not the validity of a future marriage.

APPENDICES

APPENDIX ONE

IN SEARCH OF A BALANCED PROCEDURAL LAW
FOR MARRIAGE NULLITY CASES

A. The Need For Balance

A Church tribunal is a veritable depository of tension. It fairly teems with serried conflict.

1. There is, for example, the conflict that exists between the petitioner and the respondent (and/or the defender of the bond). At the level of the individual case, every trial involves a basic controversy. There are two "sides" in every case, and those two sides come together in court as opponents or antagonists. In marriage nullity cases, as we know, the respondents themselves are not, in practice, always interested in playing the adversarial role; but always there is a defender of the bond and always, therefore, there is at least to some extent, a *proponent* and an *opponent*, a *position* and an *opposition*

The resulting tension is often quite emotional. Petitioners frequently object to the cumbersome, prolonged procedures devised, as they see it, by aloof, uncaring celibates. The requirement by the tribunal of highly detailed, highly personal information seems callous to many plaintiffs; often they have been deeply scarred by the broken marital relationship, and the relentless probing of the court seems a heartless opening of old wounds. "Why," they ask further, "does the court not accept their word as an accurate account? Why must they involve their relatives and friends as witnesses? Why must the process be so embarrassing and so painful?"

Respondents, meanwhile, are often offended by what they perceive to be the court's intrusion into their privacy. If they do eventually offer testimony, their account may differ markedly from that of the petitioner. They do not understand how the Church can annul a marriage which lasted for several years and which produced several children. They are concerned that somehow their children will be regarded in the Church as less than legitimate. They fear the besmirchment of their own reputation. They regard the court's activities as legalistic meddling.

Often, furthermore, one or both parties are not Catholic, or even Christian; they may, therefore, see a Catholic tribunal as unsympathetic, threatening, and inquisitional.

These are all real tensions, and both court personnel and the law itself must do their best to reduce them to an absolute minimum. For left untended, they can easily blind all concerned to the essential fairness and equity of the proceeding itself, the whole purpose of which, after all, is simply to settle a disputed issue in accord with the best and wisest insights of the law.

2. There is also the tension between thoroughness and expeditiousness. Since the point of every trial is to uncover not just half-truths but the "tota et sola

veritas,"[1] the pursuit of that truth must always be vigorous and complete. Innocent III expressed this idea in the phrase "Iudex . . . debet universa rimari,"[2] which has the connotation of leaving no stone unturned. The investigation, implied Innocent, should be both extensive, in that *everything* ("universa") is perused, as well as intensive, in that everything is *turned over and pried into* ("rimari").

Both Paul VI[3] and John Paul II,[4] in allocutions to the Rota, made the same point, each of them noting that the investigation should be a "complete and exhaustive" one.

At the same time, however, a trial should also be as expeditious as possible. In 1973, Pope Paul VI observed:

> You want to exercise justice with canonical equity, and you want it to be speedier, more gentle, more even tempered. As far as being speedier is concerned, it is certainly true that prudence is not necessarily to be identified with a sluggish pace, which sometimes leads to real injustice and great damage to souls."[5]

And in 1984 Pope John Paul II said:

> In reforming canonical procedural law, an effort was made to meet a very frequently uttered criticism, which is not entirely unfounded and which concerns the slowness and excessive duration of causes. . . . An effort was made to make the administration of justice more agile and functional by simplifying procedures, by expediting formalities, by shortening terms, by increasing the judge's discretional powers, etc. This effort must not be rendered vain by delaying tactics or lack of care in studying cases, by an attitude of inertia, distrustful of entering upon the new fast lanes, and by lack of professional skill in applying procedures.[6]

It is clear, therefore, that both thoroughness and expeditiousness are values to be protected in a judicial process; which means that a trial may be neither unduly prolonged for the sake of completeness nor unduly abbreviated for the sake of speed. Somehow the proper balance must be found in order to accommodate the two values.

3. Over the centuries the Church has also attempted to find the happy medium between overprotecting and underprotecting the bond of marriage. Benedict XIV certainly had a legitimate complaint in 1741 when he saw people having not just one but several marriages successively declared null by a single judge, with no defender of the bond and no appellate hearing.[7] But so did Paul VI and John Paul II when, in revising the 1917 code,[8] they modified that code's demand for at least two defenders of the bond and six judges before any marriage could be declared invalid.[9]

It seems to us now that the bond of marriage was underprotected prior to 1741 and overprotected in the years following 1917. Whether the 1983 code has, in fact, now found the proper balance between these two extremes remains, for many, an arguable point.

4. In searching for balance in protecting the bond of marriage, a middle ground must also be sought in avoiding the two extremes of laxity on the one hand and rigidity on the other. As regards laxity, Paul VI spoke out in 1976 against the position taken by some which held that marital love alone and not marital consent is constitutive of marriage, so that whenever marital love does not exist or ceases to exist, the marriage is likewise non-existent. In at least one ecclesiastical tribunal marriages were actually declared null on that "ground" (which is, of course, a non-ground) and Paul VI rightly denounced the practice[10] Two years later the same pope warned judges against "indulging in an easy-going attitude which would end up favoring permissiveness" and against granting "certain concessions as a matter of routine" which would result in "a practical evasion of the law."[11] In 1981 John Paul II spoke of how the stability of marriage and the family can be "negatively influenced by declarations or decisions of nullity when these have been obtained with too much ease."[12]

But the opposite extreme, rigidity, can also be a problem. Certain judges, for example, can be so obsessed with the evil of divorce and the disruption of family life that they are loath to declare any marriage invalid for fear that doing so will contribute to the overall disintegration of society. Such judges, therefore, will tend to apply the law with exaggerated strictness and to ignore accepted jurisprudence, and so deprive people of a hearing that is truly just and fair. Or certain judges may claim, after hearing all the evidence, that even though in their own heart and mind they are, *as people,* personally convinced that a given marriage is invalid, still the law of the Church does not, for one reason or another, permit them *as judges* to declare officially that given marriage null. Such an attitude, as Pius XII pointed out, is excessively rigid and unjustifiable. Pius wrote:

> No doubt there may at times be conflicts between "juridical formalism" and "the free weighing of the evidence," but they will usually be only apparent and hence not difficult to resolve. Now, as the objective truth is one, so too moral certainty objectively determined can be but one. Hence it is not admissible that a judge declare that personally, from the record of the case, he has moral certainty regarding the truth of the fact at issue, while at the same time, in his capacity as judge, he denies the same objective certainty on the basis of procedural law. Such contradictions should rather induce him to undertake a further and more accurate examination of the case. Not infrequently such conflicts are due to the fact that certain aspects of the case, which attain their full importance and value only when viewed as a whole, have not been properly weighed, or that the juridical-formal rules have been incorrectly understood or have been applied in a manner contrary to the mind and purpose of the legislator. In any event, the confidence of the people, which the tribunals should possess, demands that, if it is at all possible, such conflicts between the official opinion of judges and the reasonable public opinion of well educated people should be avoided and reconciled.[13]

A balance must therefore be found between rigidity on the one hand and laxity on the other, and that balance consists in flexibility, or equity, which as Paul VI pointed out, is "an attitude of mind and spirit that tempers the rigor of the law . . . and a force for proper balance in the mental process that should guide a judge in pronouncing sentence."[14]

5. A fifth tension found in tribunal work exists in the area of scholastic credentials versus experiential credentials on the part of judges, defenders of the bond, and advocates.

There is no question but that ecclesiastical tribunals, like their civil counterparts, should be run professionally. We want our courts to be sources of legitimate pride and worthy of winning the respect of all who are acquainted with them. This means, at the very least, that key court personnel should be not only kind, considerate, empathetic, well intentioned and efficient, but also that they be truly expert in their knowledge of the law and jurisprudence that bear on the settling of marriage cases.

In order to insure this end the 1917 code,[15] while preferring that the officialis, vice-officialis, defender and advocate possess a doctorate in canon law,[16] nevertheless accepted genuine expertise in the field as sufficient qualification for all judges, defenders and advocates.

The 1983 code, on the other hand, apparently feels that in the present age, a tribunal will not be truly professional unless all judges and defenders hold at least a licentiate degree,[17] though interestingly, a scholastic degree is *not* required for the advocate; it is sufficient for the advocate if he or she be "vere peritus."[18]

Everyone recognizes that much has changed since the days when Paul reminded the Corinthians that, since we Christians "are to judge the world" and "since we are also to judge angels, it follows that we can judge matters of every day life. . . . Can it be that there is no one among you wise enough to settle a case between one member of the church and another?"[19] These days more is required than simply being "wise." It is important that key personnel in church courts not be professionally underqualified. But it is probably of equal importance that the law not require that they be overqualified either. Because once a law loses its balance, it will inevitably slip. It may take some time before a loss of balance becomes noticeable, but once a law is put to the test of having to function in the real world, any imbalance that is present will, sooner or later, have negative consequences in the life of the Church.

Canon 1483 is certainly correct in noting that there are people who are "truly expert" even though they have not earned a licentiate in canon law. Every diocese of any size has at least a few such people, people who have perhaps never studied *De Bonis Temporalibus* or *De Sanctionibus,* but who know in great depth the Church's jurisprudence on marriage and who have the intelligence and wisdom to apply that jurisprudence to individual cases. The Church is no doubt right in encouraging such "experts" to assist the parties in a case as their advocates. But a law which, at the same time, disallows those same people from serving as defenders and judges (even as *one* of the judges on a collegiate tribunal) is, in the opinion of many, a law of dubious balance.

6. The matter of publicness versus confidentiality is still another area where balance is essential. Paul VI certainly stated the general principle clearly when, in a 1977 allocution, he said "a trial or process is to be, as a rule, public; and yet justice itself may require that the matter be handled secretly."[20]

Despite Pope Paul's directive, however, and despite the fact that over the last century the Church's law on the publication of the acts has been reasonably nuanced and quite well balanced, [21] the 1983 canon on the matter came perilously close to grossly overprotecting publicness and underprotecting confidentiality. The canons in both the 1976 and the 1980 drafts did exactly that and, in the judgment of many, would have been bad and harmful law.[22] Fortunately the version of the canon that was finally promulgated (C. 1598) had managed to pull out of its nosedive in the very nick of time and landed right side up. But it was a close call.

7. Several of the tensions already mentioned are heightened and exacerbated by still another tension, the one, namely, that exists between the procedure that is to be used for ordinary contentious cases on the one hand and that which is to be used for marriage cases on the other. According to the present law (C. 1425 §1, 1°) marriage cases are, in general, regarded as contentious cases and must, in general, be handled by the process which is designed for those cases (C. 1691).

There is, however, a problem here and that is that the underlying assumption of this arrangement (namely, that a marriage case should necessarily be regarded as contentious) does not reflect reality. By definition, of course, every trial involves a controversy. Not every controversy, however, involves a genuine contention. We have all seen marriage cases where the respondent does not wish to be involved and where the evidence in favor of nullity is so positively and undeniably overwhelming that the defender is in no position to contest it. Such a case (and there are many of them) should be recognized as a noncontentious controversy. It remains, perhaps, a theoretical controversy because a legal presumption in favor of validity *controverts* or formally contradicts the allegation of nullity, but the clear facts of the case itself prohibit any genuine, honest *contention* that the marriage was in fact valid.

The present law of the Church does not, however, recognize that fact. It requires, rather, that marriage cases (even though many of them are, in fact, noncontentious) follow a procedural law that was specifically and admittedly designed for contentious cases. It's like putting new wine into old wineskins. Or, to use a less biblical metaphor, it's like wearing a borrowed suit of clothes, which tends to be tight where it should be loose and loose where it should be tight. A genuinely balanced procedural law, however, consists in exactly the opposite, that is, in being tight where it should be tight and loose where it should be loose; but that kind of balance is obtained, it would seem, only from a law that is truly tailored to the specific object of the trial.

The whole purpose of canons 1671-1707, of course, is precisely to perform this tailoring task, to adjust and adapt the procedures for the ordinary contentious trial to marriage cases, but it seems legitimate to wonder whether this is not too little too late; or to put it in more biblical terms, whether it does not involve "putting a piece of unshrunken cloth on to an old cloak."

8. An eighth tension in procedural law and tribunal work is found between tradition on the one hand and innovation on the other. This, of course, is a tension that pervades all of society and life itself. But every institution and every legal system is, in a special way, constantly faced with decisions about which items in the legislative inventory should be preserved, and which should be discarded altogether or modified in favor of something better.

The procedural law of the Catholic Church has a rich and venerable tradition of which we are justifiably proud. In general, at least, it has worked and worked reasonably well for hundreds of years; it makes sense, therefore, to deal with it in accord with the old adage,"If it isn't broken, don't fix it." At the same time, however, the Church has never viewed its procedural law as etched in stone. Without ever stripping the law of its stability (an essential quality for any law), the Church has nevertheless remained ever open to reexamining its law with a view towards improving it.[23] The 1983 code is but the latest example of this.

Think, for example (and it is but one example of many), of the axiom "Actor sequitur forum rei." This was an accepted principle in classical Roman law,[24] remained so throughout the Middle Ages,[25] and was quite naturally incorporated into the Pio-Benedictine code.[26] But by the time the 1983 code was promulgated, contemporary circumstances and attitudes seemed to warrant some modification of that principle, at least as far as marriage cases were concerned. So C. 1673, 3° gracefully acknowledged that, under certain circumstances, the petitioner's domicile may also be a source of competence; that is, that sometimes the "reus [or rather the *pars conventa*] sequitur forum actoris." This was a not untypical instance of what *Sacrae disciplinae leges* called "fidelitas in novitate et novitas in fidelitate."

It should also be mentioned, though, that over the years the Church has not always been uniformly successful in excluding the bad elements (both old and new) and including the good elements (both old and new) in its body of law. Knowing which traditions to modify and which innovations to incorporate remains for each succeeding age a mighty challenge.

9. Still another tension that pervades tribunal work is the one between the common good and the individual good.

Tribunal personnel tend to look upon their work as primarily a mission to the individual people whose cases come under their purview. Jurisdictional power, as Paul VI noted, "is a pastoral power. This is to say that it is meant for service and that it looks to the good not of the person invested with the power but of those for whose sake authority is exercised."[27] It is in accord with that sentiment that courts try to give prompt, efficient, pastoral service to their clients. Tribunal work is seen basically as a ministry to individuals.

But there is another dimension to tribunal work, its contribution to the common good. Society as a whole, and especially the Catholic community, must know that within the Church there exists a judicial system that is available to all who need it, a system that follows catholic rules of evidence and catholic jurisprudence so that cases the world over will be judged according to the same basic standards.[28] Catholics should be confident that there exists, within their Church, a court system which profoundly respects the dignity and indissolubility of marriage in general, but which will nevertheless objectively and impartially investigate and adjudicate any legitimate claim that a given marriage was, for some demonstrable reason or another, invalid.

Neither the individual good nor the common good should be allowed to dominate. Excessive attention to the individual good can cause judges to become pandering and romantic while excessive concern for the common good can cause them to be insensitive and legalistic. Both "goods" or values should be protected and promoted but never to excess. Tribunals should see their work both as a ministry to persons and as a ministry to truth.

The procedural law of the Church, furthermore, should foster that approach, as indeed it does in many ways. In regard to the evaluation of evidence, for example, the 1983 code, with one eye on the common good, requires that certain standard rules of evaluation be followed (so that an allegation will be genuinely proved and not simply taken for granted); but, with the other eye on the individual good, the code sees to it that those rules are endowed with a certain flexibility (so that they can be applied with equity in individual cases). The two canons that primarily illustrate this point are the following:

> C. 1536 §2. In cases which concern the public good a judicial confession and the declarations of the parties which are not confessions can have a probative force to be evaluated by the judge along with the other circumstances of the case; but complete probative force cannot be attributed to them unless other elements are present which thoroughly corroborate them.

> C. 1573. The deposition of a single witness cannot constitute full proof unless a witness acting in an official capacity makes a deposition regarding duties performed ex officio or unless circumstances of things and persons suggest otherwise.

Both of these canons strike a nice balance and thereby provide direction to the many judges who strive to maintain that some sort of balance in their daily ministry.

10. A tenth and final example of the need for balance in procedural law can be found in the competing claims of what may be called the former marriage and the future marriage.

The *former* marriage (i.e., the one that is the object of the petition for nullity) is, as everyone knows, presumably valid. But even beyond that, the Church, according to John Paul II, is reluctant and "disinclined" to grant annulments at all. In a verbatim quotation from Pius XII,[29] John Paul II noted:

> As regards declarations of nullity of marriage, everyone knows that the Church is rather wary and disinclined to favor them. Indeed, if the tranquility, stability, and security of human intercourse in general demand that contracts be not lightly set aside, this is still more true of a contract of such importance as marriage, whose firmness and stability are necessary for the common welfare of human society as well as for the private good of the parties and the children, and whose sacramental dignity forbids that it be lightly exposed to the danger of profanation.[30]

While it may be true, in a theoretical and general sense, that the Church is "disinclined" to favor annulments, still, when in practice a court is presented with a legitimate petition for nullity, it is duty bound to proceed with that case, and should demonstrate neither disinclination nor reluctance but should rather proceed promptly, courteously, and with pastoral concern.[31] Every petitioner has a right to this.

But even beyond this basic obligation of a court to adjudicate all bona fide cases presented to it, a court must, furthermore, respect and even champion the right of the parties to enter a *future* marriage. That right exists, of course, only if the former marriage has been declared invalid, but it is precisely the court's obligation to clarify that right and to acknowledge it whenever and wherever it exists. The right to marry is a fundamental human right enjoyed by every person capable of it.[32] If, therefore, a former marriage was in fact invalid, then the parties in the case (assuming they are otherwise unimpeded) have a right to enter a future marriage. The declaration of C. 1058 to the effect that "all persons who are not prohibited by law can contract marriage" applies as much to them as to anyone else.

In practice, therefore, a typical tribunal is called upon repeatedly and perhaps even daily to respect both the right to a *future* marriage and the presumed validity (with all the ramifications mentioned by Pius and John Paul) of a *former* marriage. This, indeed, may be the most basic of all tribunal tensions.

There are, of course, other tensions[33] besides these ten to be found in the procedural law of the Church and in the work of its tribunals. But these ten can perhaps serve as a sufficient reminder of the need for constant vigilance on the part of the legislator so that the just, true and right balance will be achieved and maintained in every age and in every situation.

B. Yesterday's Search For Balance

In 1869, during the papacy of Pius IX, an article appeared in the *Acta Sanctae Sedis* urging church courts not to be apprehensive about procedural technicalities.[34] Courts should proceed confidently to hear whatever cases come to their attention, said the anonymous author, without worrying about whether a missed technicality here or there might invalidate the whole proceeding. "In curias these days," he wrote, "practically all ecclesiastical trials can be handled in summary form"[35] and, in fact, they are so handled in the pope's own courts in Rome.[36] In marriage cases, of course, certain special procedures must be followed, like the presence of a defender of the bond and a mandatory appeal;[37] but as far as judicial solemnities are concerned, their actual use is, in general, left to the discretion of the judge.[38] The article closed, finally, with these words:

> It is clear from all that has been said that the judicial canonical form is not difficult, since the form of summary judgments, by which practically all cases can be handled, amounts, when all is said and done, to that form which is demanded by the natural law and which is urged by equity.[39]

The summary procedure of which the article spoke is no longer with us. It did, however, enjoy a long and highly successful history in church law and is a prime illustration of the Church's search, over the centuries, for a balanced procedural law. The canonical origins of the summary procedure were principally in the early fourteenth century.[40] The procedure arose as a natural reaction to what was, at the time, a new rigidity in procedural law.

Prior to the Decree of Gratian (1141), as Charles Lefebvre has pointed out, judicial procedures were ruled by a mixed bag of somewhat vague principles stemming from Roman, Germanic, and canon law. This potpourri made applying the law tentative and difficult and, as a result, a *praxis paterna* developed which tended to view the various procedural directives more as guidelines than as rigid rules that had to be followed exactly.[41]

But when in the early twelfth century new methods were discovered of studying the texts of Roman law, the Roman procedural law suddenly became both quite clear and binding on church courts, and resulted in a totally untraditional procedural rigidity.[42] The Church responded to that rigidity by creating, as it were, an alternative process (which came to be called the "summary process") that would be more expeditious and more functional than the rigid and demanding ordinary process.

Boniface VIII (1294-1303), for example, allowed one case on record to be heard "sine strepitu iudicii et figura,"[43] or, as we might say "without the pomp and circumstance of a judicial proceeding." Clement V (1305-1314) issued two famous decrees, *Saepe Contingit* and *Dispendiosam,* both of which used the same "sine strepitu" phrase, and which, together, became the acknowledged constitutional foundation of the summary process.

Major cases in those days were reserved to the pope. Many such cases were delegated out to courts around the world, often with the stipulation that they be heard "sine strepitu." When, however, the precise meaning of the "sine strepitu" clause began to confuse the courts, Clement V, in 1306, issued *Saepe Contingit* in order to clarify exactly what the procedure involved. The decree read as follows:

> It often happens that we delegate lower courts to hear cases, and in some of those cases we order those courts to proceed simply and easily and without the pomp and circumstance of a judicial proceeding. The precise meaning of these words, however, is a matter of considerable debate and there is some question therefore about how courts ought to proceed.
>
> In the interest of settling as many of those questions as possible, we, by this decree, hereby declare as sacred and perpetual that a judge to whom we commit cases of this kind: need not necessarily demand a formal libellus or a joinder of issues; may proceed even on holidays in order to accommodate the needs of people who have been dispensed by the law; may shorten deadlines; may, to the extent that he can, shorten the trial by denying exceptions and dilatory and unnecessary appeals, and by restricting the contentions and disputes of the parties, advocates and procurators, and by limiting the number of witnesses.
>
> A judge may not, however, abbreviate a trial by curtailing necessary proofs or legitimate defenses. Lest the truth remain concealed, furthermore, it is understood that in commissions of this kind neither the citation nor the taking of the usual oaths of good faith and intent and to tell the truth may ever be omitted. Also, since the pronouncement of the judge ought to be based on the original petition, the plaintiff's position and that of the respondent, if he or she countersues, should be made at the beginning of the trial either in writing or orally and should always be included in the acts. This is important for three reasons: so that the investigation may be based on those petitions, so that fuller certitude may be had, and so that the issue may be more clearly defined. And because traditional judicial practice has allowed the use of questionnaires, based on the statements of the parties, for the purpose of expediting the proceedings, as well as interrogatories, for the purpose of obtaining clearer

proofs, we, wishing to follow this practice, hereby declare that any judge deputed by us (unless he proceeds otherwise at the wish of the parties) may establish a deadline for submitting these questionnaires and interrogatories as well as for all other acts and defenses which the parties wish to be used in the case. After these articles have been submitted the judge may then assign an appropriate date for producing witnesses, with the understanding, however, that should the case be interrupted, those witnesses, and documents as well, may be produced at a later date. The judge shall also question the parties either at their request or ex officio whenever equity recommends this.

Finally the judge, either standing or sitting, as he pleases, will hand down the written definitive sentence (with both parties having been cited for this action though not peremptorily) based on the petition, the proofs and other pleadings in the case. This he shall do even if, in his judgment, the evidence is not concluded.

All of which is also applicable to all those cases in which, through one or another of our constitutions, it is allowed that a judge may proceed simply and easily and without the pomp and circumstance of a judicial proceeding. But if, in these cases, the solemn judicial order is, in fact, observed, in whole or in part, with the parties not disagreeing, the process will not, on that account, be either void or voidable.[44]

Five years later, in 1311, the same pope issued *Dispendiosam*, in which he spelled out the types of cases in which the summary process could be used. It read as follows:

In the interest of reducing the lengthy delays in court trials which sometimes result, as evidence has shown, from a scrupulous application of the judicial process to individual cases, we hereby decree that regarding not only future cases but present cases as well and even those cases pending appeal, a court may proceed simply and easily and without the pomp and circumstance of a judicial proceeding in the following cases: those regarding elections, postulations, provisions, dignities, personates, offices, canonicates, revenues or any ecclesiastical benefices, the exacting of tithes (including the possibility, after a proper warning, of coercing payment by ecclesiastical censure from those who are in arrears), and finally marriage and usury cases and all those touching on them in any way.[45]

For the next six hundred years the two processes existed side by side in the Church: the ordinary process and the summary process.[46] More and more, though, the summary process prevailed and by 1869, as the article in the *Acta Sanctae Sedis* noted, practically all cases (*omnes fere causae*) were being heard in accord with it.[47]

The 1869 article noted that there were only two types of cases that could *not* be heard by the summary process, namely criminal cases of clerics, and cases involving beatification and canonization.[48] The process for these latter cases, however, has always been sui generis, and as regards the former the Congregation of Bishops and Regulars allowed, in an instruction of June 11, 1880, that even in criminal cases of clerics "processus confici potest formis summariis et absque iudicii strepitu, servatis semper regulis iustitiae substantialibus."[49]

By the beginning of the twentieth century, therefore, the Clementine process was in effect the only process being used, while the more formal ordinary process had lapsed into desuetude.[50] So one might have logically expected that the legislator of the 1917 code would simply have codified the Clementine process and then incorporated it, as is, into the code. It was, after all, the Clementine process that was, for all practical purposes, in possession.

In fact, however, that is not what happened. Instead, the legislator first resurrected, as it were, the solemn process and then took the two processes, the solemn and the summary, and made a synthesis or amalgam of them. Authors disagree as to whether the 1917 synthesis had more in common with the solemn or with the summary procedure,[51] but one thing is clear, and that is that the synthesis was considerably more solemn and formal than the Clementine process had been. It seems fair to say, therefore, that following the promulgation of the 1917 code the judicial procedure for the hearing of marriage nullity cases was more formal than it had been in at least six centuries and perhaps in the entire history of the Church.[52]

But there was more. Besides demanding extra formalities in judicial procedures, the Pio-Benedictine code introduced a new rigidity that was not unlike the rigidity of the thirteenth century, except perhaps that it was more centralized. No longer could it be said, as the 1869 *Acta* article had said,

> the words "canonical form" are highly equivocal and can have as many meanings as there are styles of judging in legitimate tribunals: for all tribunals customarily have their own special form of proceeding, either by reason of an old and legitimate custom or by reason of special laws imposed on them; all of which is especially evident in Rome itself; and all of these forms are worthily called "canonical."[53]

After the Pio-Benedictine code was promulgated there was only one procedural form, namely the form that was entitled *De Iudiciis in genere*, which comprised canons 1556 to 1924. It was all quite formal and was so scrupulously applied by courts around the world that it paralyzed many of them. In the United States, for example, a survey of the Latin Rite dioceses showed that in the year 1968 (fifty years after the effective date of the code), 60 tribunals gave no sentences at all, 20 more tribunals gave only one, and 19 more gave only two; only 17 tribunals of the 130 reporting (out of a possible 145) gave more than five decisions and only 1 tribunal gave more than thirty.[54]

In that same year, 1968, however, there was a reaction to this rigidity. Once again a balance was sought. In November of that year the National Conference of Catholic Bishops in the United States voted to study and comment on the newly drafted *American Procedural Norms*, and in April of 1969 the same conference voted to propose the norms to the Holy See for approval. Approval was granted and the norms went into effect in the United States in 1970 and remained in effect for the next thirteen years.

The *American Procedural Norms* were very much in the spirit of *Saepe Contingit* and *Dispendiosam*. The content, of course, was quite different (it was a different age), but the spirit was very similar. It was a spirit in search of a judicial procedure that could be conducted "simpliciter et de plano, ac sine strepitu iudicii et figura." It was a spirit in search of balance.

When Paul VI issued *Causas matrimoniales* in 1971, he, to some extent at least, passed the spirit on to the rest of the world; both of these documents, *Causas matrimoniales* and (in a less direct way) the *American Procedural Norms,* influenced the drafting of the new procedural law. As in the 1917 code, however, a marriage case in the 1983 code is perceived as a contentious case (C. 1425 §1, 1°) and the marriage process follows, in general, the rules for the ordinary and contentious process (C. 1691).

The ordinary contentious process of the 1983 code incorporates most, if not all, of the specific relaxations of the old Clementine process, and in that sense, perhaps, it qualifies as an accurate reflection of the old summary process.[55] Two points, however, should be made here. First, since specific elements change with the times (and the times have changed a great deal since 1306), perhaps a more accurate test of whether the present ordinary contentious process should or should not be classified as "summary" is not to compare the specific elements of the 1983 document with those of the 1306 document, but rather to look to Wernz' description (the summary process contains only those elements required by the *natural* law and omits those required by *human law*)[56] or to Lega's (*the summary process contains only the necessary* elements and omits those that are merely *useful*)[57] and then to ask whether these descriptions really apply to our present ordinary contentious process. The second point is that when all is said and done, the real question is not whether the new procedural law of the Church is Clementine but whether it is clement. The question is not whether our law fits the *letter* of the *old* summary process; the question, rather, is whether our law is inspired with the *spirit* of balance, and is thus prepared to meet the *present* needs of our people.

C. Today's Search For Balance

Since practically all of the cases heard in church courts today are marriage cases,[58] the primary procedural need in our time is for a process that is truly suited to the hearing of these cases. The question, then, is whether our present procedural law is a reasonably effective instrument for investigating and adjudicating the many claims of marriage nullity that come to the attention of our courts.

The basic structure for the processing of marriage cases under the 1983 code is the same as that of the 1917 code. In both codes, marriage cases are ruled first of all by several hundred canons on trials in general and then by a handful of canons on marriage processes in particular.

In the years following the promulgation of the 1917 code, it was discovered that this system worked poorly. There were two basic problems with the system. The first was that local tribunals found it difficult to be trying constantly to apply the general procedural norms to marriage cases. Indeed, the stated purpose of the 1936 Instruction, *Provida Mater Ecclesia,* was precisely to correct this problem. The second paragraph of *Provida* noted:

> experience has shown that the judges of diocesan curiae, when they come to apply the procedural laws, especially the general ones, to particular cases, sometimes encounter many difficulties.[59]

But besides the problem of having to apply the general norms to particular types of cases, like marriage cases, there was the second problem of having to apply a contentious process to non-contentious cases. Vittorio Bartocetti, in his commentary on *Provida,* noted that there is a big difference between marriage cases and contentious cases,[60] and it was this difference, he said, that was the principal reason why local judges were having problems prior to *Provida.* "There are" said Bartocetti

> many difficulties in fitting rules, especially procedural rules, to particular cases. This will appear inevitable to anyone who thinks about the very special nature of a marriage process which, as we have seen, can not be perfectly identified with a purely contentious process. . . .[61]

Given the "many difficulties" mentioned by both *Provida* and Bartocetti, and given the fact that the source of those difficulties had been identified as the basic structure of the 1917 procedural law, one would have expected that in revising that law, the 1983 code would have avoided repeating the same mistake. In fact, however, the *De Processibus* coetus decided, in its wisdom, that all things considered, it would be best to follow the basic procedural format of the Pio-Benedictine code.[62]

That decision of the coetus was, in the minds of many, a most unfortunate one, mostly because once again, it has left the tribunals of the world, which deal almost exclusively with marriage cases, without a process specifically designed for those cases. The tribunals of the world are once again being asked to "made do" with a process that is fundamentally ill-suited to their work.

It could be argued, of course, that enough specific improvements have been made in the 1983 code to insure that there will be no repetition of the post-1917 experience. But the problem is more fundamental than that. The problem is that the whole tone of a contentious process is wrong for a marriage case, especially an open-and-shut one that is completely uncontested, and all the tinkering in the world is not going to correct that problem. True balance is never achieved that way.

It would seem, therefore, that the only solution now is for the Church to issue, just as it did in 1936, a new piece of legislation, legislation that will regulate the procedure to be followed by courts in adjudicating marriage cases. What is needed, however, is not just another *Provida,* because as Doheney noted, *Provida* was merely "a coordinated restatement of the rulings of the Code on matrimonial procedure."[63] *Provida,* in other words, accepted and implicitly endorsed the premise that the contentious process and the matrimonial process were basically compatible, and so for the most part it merely took the existing contentious process and "matri-monialized" it, so to speak. That approach, however, left the underlying problem untouched, and *Provida* therefore turned out to be an exquisitely crafted non-solution. The tribunals of the world remained just as catatonic after it as they were before. This is not what we need today.

What we need today is a complete procedural law designed from top to bottom for marriage cases. This does not mean, of course, that the great wisdom to be found in the Church's traditional process would be ignored. But it does mean that we could start with a clean slate, free of any artificial encumbrances imposed from without.

To draft a complete procedural law from start to finish with only marriage cases in mind would be no easy task. Such a law would have to achieve over and over again that often elusive and delicate balance between all those competing values and sometimes seductive extremes that pervade tribunal work, some examples of which were mentioned in the first section of this article. But starting from scratch would, at least, have the very great advantage of allowing the legislator first to take the full and exact measure of a marriage case (weighing its specific nature and all its complexities), and then to fashion for it a truly tailor-made process — which marriage cases certainly deserve.

Such a process would, among other things, probably address such questions as: Should a marriage process be absolutely universal in every detail or should local circumstances be allowed to prevail in certain areas? What rights should be enjoyed by a respondent who, with the purely spiteful intention of depriving the petitioner of the sacraments, refuses to cooperate in a first instance proceeding? Are there any conditions under which a defender would be permitted to argue not *pro vinculo* but *pro rei veritate*? Under what circumstances should a defender appeal a first instance affirmative decision? Is the ratification process (many feel it has already deteriorated into mere formalism) really workable? Is it really necessary to involve four judges and (usually) two defenders before any marriage case, even the simplest, can be finally settled? Is it really necessary for all judges and defenders to have scholastic degrees (there are indications already that some canon law schools, largely because of this requirement, are lowering their standards for the licentiate, the overall effect of which would certainly be damaging)? Should there be such a thing as curable nullity? Under what conditions should guardians and curators be appointed? Under what conditions can the *caput nullitatis* be changed, even minimally, during the course of a trial? Must the names of witnesses always be submitted to the parties? In what areas should tribunals be protected from civil subpoenas and suits? Does the respondent always have the right to read the sentence? Do the parties have an absolute right to appeal a first instance decision to the Rota? When is a third instance hearing permitted apart from the Rota?

These questions and a host of others should be answered by a new matrimonial process which would be drafted within the context of a consistent, balanced philosophy and theology regarding the sacrament of matrimony in general and the right of a spouse, in a particular instance, to allege the nullity of a given marriage. That and only that should be the complete and total context within which the process would be drafted.

With such a process in place, the situation would be not unlike that which existed prior to the 1917 code; i.e., we would have, for all practical purposes, two side-by-side processes: the ordinary process (which would be used rather rarely), and an extraordinary process (a marriage process, actually, which would be used in almost all cases heard by tribunals).[64] The objection could be raised that this would, in effect, put us back to the turn of the century, and, in a sense, that is true. But it is also true that a return to the past is not always bad.

ENDNOTES

1   1983 Code, C. 1530 and C. 1562. §1.
2   X, 2, 22, 10.
3   Paul VI, allocution of January 28, 1978, *AAS* 70 (1978) 182; CLD 9; 921.
4   John Paul II, allocution of January 24, 1981: *AAS* 73 (1981) 232; CLD 9, 946. See also the allocution of February 4, 1980; *AAS* 72 (1980) 175; CLD 9, 937.
5   Paul VI, allocution of February 8, 1973: *AAS* 65 (1973) 103: *The Pope Speaks [TPS]* 18 (1973) 82.
6   John Paul II, allocution of January 26, 1984: *AAS* 76 (1984) 647: *Origins* 13, 35 (1984) 584.

7   Benedict XIV, *Dei Miseratione, Fontes* n. 318, 1: 695-701.

8   Paul VI by *Causas matrimoniales*, John Paul II by the 1983 code.

9   1917 code, cc. 1576 §1, 1°; 1586; 1986 and 1987.

10 Paul VI, allocution of February 9, 1976: *AAS* 68 (1976) 204-208; *CLD* 8: 790-795.

11 Paul VI, allocution of January 28, 1978: *AAS* 70 (1978) 183; *CLD* 9: 922.

12 John Paul II, allocution of January 24, 1981: *AAS* 73 (1981) 231; *CLD* 9: 945.

13 Pius XII, allocution of October 1, 1942: *AAS* 34 (1942) 341-342; *CLD* 3: 609-610.

14 Paul VI, allocution of February 8, 1973: *AAS* 65 (1973) 99; *TPS* 18 (1973) 79.

15 1917 code, cc. 1573 §4; 1574 §1; 1589 §1; 1657 §2.

16 The 1917 code did not expect synodal and prosynodal judges to hold scholastic degrees. Cf. c. 1574 §1.

17 1983 code, cc. 1420 §4; 1421 §3; 1435.

18 1983 code, c. 1483.

19 I. Cor. 6: 1-6.

20 Paul VI, allocution of February 4, 1977: *AAS* 69 (1977) 152; *CLD* 8: 110.

21 Lawrence G. Wrenn in *The Code of Canon Law: A Text and Commentary;* ed. James A. Coriden et al, (New York/Mahwah: Paulist, 1985), pp. 991-992.

22 John G. Proctor, "Procedural Change in the 1983 Code: The Experience of the Ecclesiastical Provinces of California," *The Jurist* 44 (1984) 475-476.

23 For some reflections by Paul VI on this topic, see his allocution of January 28, 1971: *AAS* 53 (1971) 139; *TPS* 16 (1971) 76.

24 *Corpus Iuris Civilis, Codex,* III, XIII, 2.

25 C. III, q. 6. c. 16; C. XI, q. 1. c. 15, 16, 45; X, II, 2, 8.

26 1917 code, c. 1559 §3.

27 Paul VI, allocution of January 30, 1975: *AAS* 67 (1975) 179-180; *TPS* 20 (1975) 83.

28 1983 code, c. 221.

29 Pius XII, allocution of October 3, 1941: *AAS* 33 (1941) 423; *CLD* 2: 456.

30 John Paul II, allocution of January 24, 1981: *AAS* 73 (1981) 232; *CLD* 9: 945-946.

31 See, for example, cc. 1453 and 1505 §1.

32 X, IV, I, 23.

33 Should defenders, for example, argue "pro rei veritate" or "pro validitate matrimonii"? The answer, of course, is that they should do both. See Pius XII's allocution of October 2, 1944: *AAS* 36 (1944) 285; English text in Appendix Five on p. 121. Or, to take another, much more fundamental, example, should Christians be seeking a legal ruling in order to determine their freedom to marry, or should they rather be following the Spirit? St. Paul seemed to suggest a genuine tension here when he wrote, "If you are guided by the Spirit you are not under the law" (Gal. 5:18). A vast body of literature has sought to find the balanced response to this question.

34 "De Potestate Ecclesiastica Iudicandi deque Iudiciis Summariis," *ASS* 5 (1869) 35-48.

35 Ibid., p. 39.

36 Ibid., pp. 43-46.

37 Ibid., p. 47.

38 Ibid., p. 47.

39 Ibid. p. 48.

40 For its more remote origins in Roman and canon law see Charles Lefebvre, "Les Origines Romaines de la Procedure Sommaire aux XII et XIII s.," *Ephemerides Iuris Canonici* 12 (1956) 149-197.

41 Charles Lefebvre, "De Iudicio Reddendo in Ecclesia (Lineamenta Historica)." *Monitor Ecclesiasticus* (1976) 226, 228.

42 Ibid., p. 228.

43 VI, I, 6, 43.

44 Clem. V, II, 2.

45 Clem. II, 1, 2.

46 The summary process was exactly the process described by Clement V and has, indeed, been referred to as the "Clementine process." F. X. Wernz in his pre-code manual *Ius Decretalium* (Prati, 1914), defined a summary trial as "a trial in which the solemnities required by the natural law are observed while those formalities which retard the expeditious pace of the proceeding and which are required only by human law are omitted" (5: 568). Wernz, pp. 570-572, listed six elements which could be *omitted* in the summary process (e.g., the written libellus) and five elements which had to be *retained* (e.g., necessary proofs), all of which were taken directly from *Saepe Contingit.*

47 Wernz, pp. 572-573, listed eight different categories of cases that could be handled by the Clementine process, including the cases of poor people, cases requiring an expeditious hearing because of some imminent danger, and of course, marriage cases.

48 *ASS* 5 (1869) 39.

49 *Fontes* 6: 1023, art. 10.

50 M. Lega. Vittorio Bartocetti, *Commentarius in Iudicia Ecclesiastica* (Rome, 1938) 2: 964, note 4.

51 Zenon Grocholewski, "Natura ed Oggetto del Processo Contenzioso Sommario," *Ephemerides Iuris Canonici* 34 (1978) 117-119.

52 It should also be noted that whereas before the 1917 code, marriage cases could be heard by a single judge (see, for example, *Causae Matrimoniales,* nn. 6, 9, and 24 in *Fontes* 7: 480, 482-483), the 1917 code itself (c. 1576 §1, 1°) required a college of three judges. Before the 1917 code, in other words, a single judge could follow the Clementine process; after the code, a college of judges had to follow the ordinary process.

Perhaps it should also be remembered that in the United States and other mission territories, prior to 1884 when *Causae Matrimoniales* was promulgated, marriage cases were often heard by a local priest, without any judicial formalities at all.

53 *ASS* 5 (1869) 38.

54 Lawrence Wrenn, "The American Procedural Norms," *The American Ecclesiastical Review* 165 (1971) 178.

55 Besides the *ordinary* contentious process, the 1983 code also contains an *oral* contentious process, which was indeed called the *summary* contentious process in the 1976 draft. The oral process, however, is both more liberal and more conservative than the Clementine process. It is more liberal in that it is extremely simple and expeditious; it is more conservative in that it can be utilized in only a few types of cases. In a 1979 meeting of the *De Processibus coetus,* as a matter of fact, one of the consultors suggested that the oral process should be suppressed since it would hardly ever be used; *Communicationes* II (1979) 248. For a thorough commentary on the oral contentious process see I. Madero, "El Proceso Contencioso oral en el Codex Iuris Canonici de 1983," *Ius Canonicum* (1984) 197-291.

56 See above, note 46.

57 M. Lega, *Praelectiones de Iudiciis Ecclesiasticis* (Rome, 1905) 1: 65.

58 *Communicationes* 10 (1978) 211: 11 (1979) 67, 80-81, 134, 152. See also *Statistical Yearbook of the Church 1981* (Vatican City: Officium Statisticum), p. 335.

59 *CLD* 2: 471; *AAS* 28 (1936) 313.

60 Vittorio Bartocetti, *De Causis Matrimonialibus* (Rome, 1950) p. 5.

61 Ibid., p. 12.

62 *Communicationes* 6 (1974) 39-41; 10 (1978) 209-212.

63 William Doheny, *Canonical Procedure in Matrimonial Cases: Formal Judicial Procedure* (Milwaukee: Bruce, 1938), p. 3.

64 As observed above in footnote 55, it is anticipated that the oral contentious process will be used only minimally, at least for the foreseeable future.

APPENDIX TWO

NORMS FOR INTERDIOCESAN, REGIONAL
OR
INTERREGIONAL TRIBUNALS

Issued by the Apostolic Signatura - December 28, 1970

CHAPTER 1

Decision to Establish Tribunals

Art. 1

§1. In order that the handling of judicial cases, especially marriage cases, may be taken care of with greater care and speed, there should be had in the Church interdiocesan, regional or interregional tribunals. Their establishment is provided for by the Supreme Tribunal of the Apostolic Signatura either at the request of the bishops concerned, including those of the Oriental Churches, or also, if the case so warrants, at the decision of the said Supreme Tribunal of the Apostolic Signatura.

§2. The establishment, constitution and method of procedure of these tribunals are governed by the following norms without prejudice to the law of the Oriental Churches.

Art. 2

§1. If the establishment is made at the request of the bishops, the bishops concerned, after having sought and received the "nothing hinders" of the Supreme Tribunal of the Apostolic Signatura, draw up the decree of establishment which, however, will not have force except after approval by the Holy See.

§2. In order to request the "nothing hinders," the bishops concerned, united in their respective assembly, must agree among themselves and report to the Supreme Tribunal of the Apostolic Signatura:

1) on the reasons why they stipulated that tribunals must be established.

2) on the trials or cases for which these tribunals are being established, sc., whether for marriage cases only, whether of nullity or of separation, or also for cases of rights and for criminal cases.

3) on the number of tribunals to be established for first and second instance, with clear indication of the dioceses (with their own proper "curial" name) for whose territory the common tribunal of first and second instance is to be constituted.

4) on the seat and territory of each kind of tribunal together with a geographical map on which is described what is sought for under art. 2, §2, n. 3).

§3. As often as there is question of regional tribunals, the *assembly* mentioned in §2 is the respective episcopal conference and the decision must be passed by at least two-thirds of the votes in accord with the decree, *Christus Dominus,* n. 38, 4. On the other hand, if there is question of interdiocesan tribunals which are not regional, the *assembly* is understood as the meeting of the bishops concerned who, indeed, must be unanimous regarding the individual points indicted above.

§4. In the executory letter of decree of establishment referred to in art. 2, §1, mention should be made of the approbation of the Holy See.

Art. 3

If the establishment takes place at the instigation and decision of the Apostolic Signatura, this tribunal will proceed according to its own usage and practice.

CHAPTER 2

The Moderator, Judges and Officers of the Tribunals

Art. 4

The interdiocesan, regional, interregional tribunal is under the authority of the diocesan bishop of the place where it is located, or, if the episcopal see is vacant, of the senior bishop of the respective circuit. This bishop, inasmuch as he is the moderator of the tribunal, governs it in the name of all the bishops for whose territory it was constituted and to him belong all the rights and duties which, according to the sacred canons, belong to local Ordinaries relative to their own tribunal. This also holds regarding cases of nullity of marriage in accord with the instruction, *Provida Mater,* of the Sacred Congregation for the Discipline of the Sacraments, 15 August, 1936, unless some other special provision has been made or the matter under consideration clearly so demands.

Art. 5

§1. The officialis, judges, promoter of justice, defender of the bond, as well as their substitutes are appointed by an absolute majority of the votes which must be cast in the common assembly of the bishops of the respective territorial circuit for which the tribunal has been established.

§2. The other officers are appointed by the tribunal moderator in accord with common law.

§3. The nomination of the officialis, judges, promoter of justice, and defender of the bond should be made known to the Supreme Tribunal of the Apostolic Signatura.

Art. 6

All the aforesaid persons:

1. should, as a rule, possess the rank of priests, be outstanding in integrity, and, at least as far as judges are concerned, have a doctorate in canon law.

2. should really possess judicial learning and experience.

3. should be able to spend the necessary amount of time in the proper discharge of the duty conferred on them.

Art. 7

They are obliged to take an oath before the moderator or his delegate regarding the due and faithful discharge of their office.

Art. 8

§1. The officialis, judges, promoter of justice, defender of the bond (as well as their substitutes, unless the latter were deputed by way of act) cannot be removed from office except for a serious reason and by the respective common assembly of bishops in the same way in which they were appointed.

§2. On the other hand, in a case of urgent necessity, the tribunal moderator himself can suspend them but should provide for their removal or substitution according to art. 5, §1 of these norms.

§3. The Apostolic Signatura must always, however, be told of the removal.

Art. 9

§1. No one can perform the function of judge who shall have exercised the function of advocate or procurator in the same tribunal or is actually exercising such function in any other tribunal, whether directly or by substitute.

§2. The same thing holds true regarding the promoter of justice and the defender of the bond.

§3. All those mentioned in art. 8 are strictly forbidden to inject themselves in any way whatever into any kind of case outside their assignment.

Art. 10

After having taken counsel with the other bishops of the respective territorial circuit, the tribunal moderator should draw up a register of advocates and procurators with regard to whom the prescriptions of cc. 1655-1666 must be observed and, likewise, if they must exercise their duty in cases of nullity of marriage, the prescriptions of articles 47, §4; 48, §§2-4; 53, §2 of the aforesaid instruction, *Provida Mater.*

CHAPTER 3

Manner of Procedure in Handling of Cases

Art. 11

In the handling of cases the prescriptions of law should be accurately observed but with the additions and changes stipulated below.

Art. 12

The bill of complaint should be laid before the moderator of the competent tribunal.

Art. 13

Cases should be registered as follows: first, there should be placed the name of the tribunal, namely, regional or interdiocesan or interregional; then the name of the diocese in whose tribunal the case should have been handled in first instance according to the common law; in the last place, the title of the case; for example, Florence, that is, Pistoia. Nullity of marriage (N. N.); Lyon, that is, Grenoble. Nullity of marriage (N. N.).

Art. 14

§1. It will belong to the tribunal moderator to admit or to designate a tutor or guardian in accord with cc. 1648 and 1651 and without prejudice to art. 78, §3 of the above-mentioned instruction, *Provida Mater.*

§2. With regard to a procurator for minors, however, the prescription of C. 1648, §3 should be observed.

§3. On the other hand, the said moderator will decide these matters after having taken counsel with the Ordinary of the party for whom a tutor or guardian or procurator is to be appointed.

Art. 15

The local Ordinary referred to in articles 37-41 of the instruction, *Provida Mater,* must be understood as the Ordinary of domicile of the spouses. But before he passes his own judgment, he shall opportunely deal with the tribunal moderator.

Art. 16

§1. In the exceptional cases provided for in cc. 1990-1992, every petition should be remitted to the tribunal moderator who, after having obtained the opinion of the bishop of domicile of the spouses, should review it in accordance with articles 226-231 of the above-cited instruction, *Provida Mater.*

§2. Likewise, the officialis referred to in art. 228 is the officialis of the said tribunal.

CHAPTER 4

Remuneration for Tribunal Officers, Advocates and Procurators; Fees and Judicial Expenses

Art. 17

Remuneration for the judges and officers should be determined in the assembly of the bishops of the respective territorial circuit after having considered well the circumstances of the assignments, places and times and the number of cases.

Art. 18

§1. In the same way and according to the same norm there should be determined a list of the fees and judicial expenses and of the emoluments pertinent to advocates and procurators.

§2. That kind of list, however, must be made clearly known to the litigants from the moment the introductory bill of complaint is exhibited.

Art. 19

Whenever gratuitous or semi-gratuitous legal assistance has been conceded, the burden of meeting the expenses devolves upon the fund set up by the respective assembly of bishops.

Art. 20

The same assembly shall decide in what measure or proportion each one of the dioceses shall provide assistance to the respective tribunals of first and second instance, both by supplying suitable priests for the assignments as judges and officers, and by paying a monetary contribution from which as well as from the entrance money of the tribunals the stipends of persons and the costs of each tribunal can be paid.

CHAPTER 5

Temporary or Transitory Norms

Art. 21

The decree, whereby interdiocesan or regional or interregional tribunals of either first or second instance are constituted and which has been approved by the Holy See, should be committed to execution as soon as possible by the president of the episcopal conference on a date to be determined by himself.

Art. 22

With regard to cases which, on the date of execution of the decree, are pending in the ordinary diocesan tribunals of the respective territorial circuit, these norms shall be observed:

1. Cases which are being acted upon in first instance, should be turned over to the new tribunal of first instance if the issues have not yet been defined in accordance with common law; cases, however, which look to nullity of marriage and are only in the initiatory stage can be turned over to the same tribunal if the consent of each of the spouses and of the defender of the bond is obtained.

On the other hand, if the decree of closing in the case has been already declared and issued, the definitive sentence must be pronounced by the tribunal before which the case was introduced.

In each case appeal is lodged with the new appellate tribunal, without prejudice, however, to the faculty referred to in C. 1599, §1, n. 1.

2. With the appropriate changes having been made, the same procedure should be followed in cases which are being acted upon in the appellate level.

The present norms shall obtain their full and entire effects on the feast of the Annunciation of B.V.M., that is, on the 25th day of March, 1971.

Given at Rome, at the seat of the Supreme tribunal of the Apostolic Signatura, the 28th day of December, 1970.

PETRINE PRIVILEGE
INSTRUCTION AND NORMS

Issued by the Congregation for the Doctrine of the Faith - December 6, 1973.

GENERAL NORMS

As is well known, this S. Congregation has for a rather long time been treating of and studying the question of dissolution of marriage in favor of the faith.

Now, at least, after the matter has been diligently investigated, His Holiness, Pope Paul VI, has deigned to approve these new norms in which are declared the conditions for a grant of dissolution of marriage in favor of the faith, whether the petitioner is baptized or is a convert or is not.

I.   In order that a dissolution may be validly granted, *three* conditions are *absolutely (sine quibus non)* required:

a) lack of baptism of one of the two spouses during the whole time of their married life;

b) nonuse of the marriage after the baptism perchance received by the party who was not baptized;

c) that the person who is not baptized or baptized outside the Catholic Church yields freedom and ability to the Catholic party to profess his own religion and to baptize and educate the children as Catholics; this condition must be safeguarded in the form of a promise (*cautio*).

II.   It is further required:

§1. that there is no possibility of restoring married life because of persistent radical and irremediable discord.

§2. that from the grant of favor no danger of public scandal or serious wonderment be had.

§3. that the petitioner is not the culpable cause of the wreckage of the valid, non-sacramental marriage and the Catholic party with whom the new marriage is to be contracted or convalidated, did not provoke separation of the spouses by reason of fault on his own part.

§4. that the other party of the previous marriage be interpellated if possible, and does not offer reasonable opposition.

§5. that the party seeking the dissolution take care that children who may have been born of the previous marriage be brought up in a religious manner.

§6. that equitable provisions be made according to the laws of justice for the abandoned spouse and for the children who may have been generated.

§7. that the Catholic party with whom a new marriage is to be entered live in accord with his baptismal promises and take care of the new family.

§8. that when there is a question of a catechumen with whom marriage is to be contracted, moral certitude be had regarding the baptism to be received shortly, if the baptism itself cannot be waited for (which is to be encouraged).

III. Dissolution is more readily granted if on some other ground there is serious doubt about the validity of the marriage itself. *This is why they gave the Fresno.*

IV. A marriage between a Catholic party and a party not baptized entered into with a dispensation from disparity of cult can also be dissolved provided that the conditions set down in nn. II and III are verified and provided that the Catholic party, because of the particular circumstances of the region, especially because of the very small number of Catholics in the region, cannot avoid marriage and cannot live a life consonant with the Catholic religion in the said marriage. Moreover, this S. Congregation must be instructed about the publicity of the marriage celebrated.

V. Dissolution of a valid, non-sacramental marriage entered into with a dispensation from the impediment of disparity of cult is not granted to a Catholic party who petitions to enter a new marriage with a non-baptized person who is not a convert.

VI. Dissolution of a valid, non-sacramental marriage is not granted if it was contracted or convalidated after a dissolution had been obtained from a previous valid non-sacramental marriage.

In order that these conditions may be duly met, *"new procedural norms"* have been drawn up. All future processes must be instructed according to them. These norms are appended to the present instruction.

These new norms completely abrogate the previous norms which were passed for the instruction of these processes.

PROCEDURAL NORMS

Art. 1

The local Ordinary who is competent according to the prescription of the apostolic letter, *Causas matrimoniales,* IV, §1, either personally or through another ecclesiastic delegated by him, draws up the process permitting concession of the favor of dissolution of a valid, non-sacramental marriage. There must be proof of the conferred delegation or commission in the acts which are to be transmitted to the Holy See.

Art. 2

Deductions must not be simply stated but also proved according to the prescriptions of canon law, either by documents or by depositions made by trustworthy witnesses.

Art. 3

Documents exhibited both in their original form and in authentic copy must be recognized personally by the Ordinary or the delegated judge.

Art. 4

§1. In the preparation of the questions which must be proposed to the parties and to the witnesses, the services of the defender of the bond or of another person delegated in each case for the discharge of this role must be used. Mention of this delegation must be made in the acts.

§2. Before witnesses are interrogated, they must take an oath to tell the truth.

§3. The Ordinary or his delegate should propose the questions already prepared and should add others he judges appropriate for better cognizance of the matter or which the very responses already given suggest.

When the parties or the witnesses make depositions about facts which are not firsthand, the judge should also interrogate about the source or origin of their knowledge.

§4. The judge must take diligent care that the questions and the responses given are accurately written down by the notary and subscribed to by the witness.

Art. 5

§1. If a given witness is a non-Catholic and refuses to present himself and make a deposition before a Catholic priest, a document containing the deposition made concerning this matter before a notary public or other trustworthy person may be accepted. This fact must be noted in express terms in the acts.

§2. In order to decide whether faith is to be put in this document, the Ordinary or delegated judge should bring in sworn witnesses, especially Catholic, who know the non-Catholic witness well and who will and are able to give testimony regarding his veracity.

§3. The judge himself should also express his opinion concerning the faith to be put in this document.

Art. 6

§1. The lack of baptism of one of the two spouses must be so demonstrated that all prudent doubt is removed.

§2. The spouse who himself says he has been baptized [sic] should, if possible, be interrogated under oath.

§3. Moreover, witnesses should be sought out, especially the spouse's parents and blood relatives and other persons, particularly those who attended him during infancy and have known his whole course of life.

§4. Witnesses must be interrogated not solely about the lack of baptism but also about the circumstances from which it may appear both credible and probable that baptism was not conferred.

§5. Care must be taken that the baptismal records be consulted in the places where the party who is said to be unbaptized lived his infancy; and especially in the churches which the party frequented to acquire his religious training or in which he celebrated his marriage.

Art. 7

§1. If at the time at which the favor of dissolution is requested the spouse who was not baptized has already been admitted to baptism, a process, at least in summary form, must be instituted, with the intevention of the defender of the bond, regarding the nonuse of the marriage after the baptism thus received.

§2. The spouse himself should be interrogated under oath whether, after separation from his spouse, he had any and what kind of relation with his spouse and, particularly, whether after baptism he had marital contacts with his partner.

§3. However, the other party will also have to be interrogated under oath, if possible, regarding the nonconsummation of the marriage.

§4. Furthermore, witnesses, especially from the blood relatives and from friends, must be brought in and heard, also under oath, not only concerning those matters which occurred after the separation of the parties and, particularly, after baptism, but also concerning the probity and veracity of the spouses, that is, concerning the faith which their depositions merit.

Art. 8

If the petitioner is a convert and baptized, he should be interrogated about the time and the intent which led him to reception of baptism or to conversion.

Art. 9

§1. In the said case, the judge should interrogate the pastor and other priests who were involved in presenting the teaching of the faith to him and in preparing his conversion. They should be interrogated about the reasons which led the petitioner to receive baptism.

§2. The Ordinary shall never send a petition to the S. Congregation for the Doctrine of the Faith unless every kind of reasonable suspicion regarding the sincerity of conversion has been removed.

Art. 10

§1. The ordinary or the delegated judge shall interrogate the petitioner and the witnesses about the cause of the separation or divorce, that is, was it placed by the petitioner or not.

§2. The judge should append to the acts an authentic copy of the divorce.

Art. 11

The judge or the Ordinary should report whether from the marriage or from the concubinage the petitioner generated children and how he will provide or intends to provide for their religious education.

Art. 12

The judge or Ordinary should likewise report how the petitioner has made plans or intends to plan equitably, in accord with the laws of justice, for the abandoned spouse and children who may have been born.

Art. 13

The Ordinary or the delegated judge should gather information concerning the non-Catholic spouse from which it will be able to be deduced whether a restoration of married life can be hoped for. He should not fail to report whether the non-Catholic party has attempted a new marriage after the divorce.

Art. 14

In express terms the Ordinary should report whether, if the favor should be granted, any danger of scandal, wonderment or calumnious interpretation is to be feared among both Catholics and non-Catholics as though by its practice the Church favored the use of divorce. Moreover, the circumstances should be set forth which render the danger probable in the instance or exclude its probability.

Art. 15

The Ordinary should express in each case the reasons which recommend the grant of the favor and, at the same time, always add whether the petitioner has in any way already attempted a new marriage or is living in concubinage. The said Ordinary should make an accurate report on the fulfillment of the conditions for concession of the favor and whether the promises referred to in n. I, under letter c) have been made; an authentic copy of them should be sent.

Art. 16

The Ordinary should send to the S. Congregation for the Doctrine of Faith three copies of the petition and all the acts and reports for all of which he is held responsible.

SOME NOTES ON THE PETRINE PRIVILEGE

A. The Term

The earliest demonstrable use of the term "Petrine Privilege" was by Franz Hürth, S.J. in his unpublished 1946 class notes for use at the Gregorian University. It was by reason of these notes that Hürth has been credited with having *coined* the term.

A decade later Hürth went public with the term in an article published in *Periodica* entitled "Notae Quaedam Ad Privilegium Petrinum" and, in so doing, he *popularized* the term. As Navarrete noted:

> Before this article few authors used the term; after it, many did and all of them cited Hürth, even if they disagreed with him in his definition of a Petrine Privilege.[1]

Among the "many" authors who used the term in the 1950s and 1960s were Abate, Alonso, Bánk, Bender, Bride, Buijs, Coronata, Fanfani, Gortebecke-Beyer, Iorio, Monserrat, Mörsdorf, Wenner and Zalba. Not all of them, as Navarrete observed, took kindly to the term.[2]

But despite the considerable opposition to the term, and despite the fact that there has never been any official recognition of it, the term nevertheless has caught on and held on. It did so because it was reasonably accurate and extremely useful.

It was reasonably accurate. The only marriage that *cannot* "be dissolved by any human power or for any reason other than death" is the marriage between two baptized people that is consummated.[3] One may conclude from this that, as far as the baptismal status of the parties is concerned, the following marriages *can* be dissolved: (a) the marriage of two unbaptized people, one of whom converts; (b) the marriage of two unbaptized people, neither of whom converts; (c) the marriage of two people, one of whom is unbaptized and the other baptized. The *Pauline* Privilege is applicable, as C. 1143, §1 indicates, only in situation a. If, therefore, the marriages described under b. and c. are to be dissolved (and, as C. 1141 suggests, they are dissoluble), it is done by what is known as the *Petrine* Privilege. By making that observation one does not, of course, magically and automatically create a highly precise definition of the Petrine Privilege. At the same time, however, the observation does describe the general ambit of the Petrine Privilege, and many canonists have found that description as well as the term itself reasonably accurate.

The term is also an extremely useful one. The marriage described above under situation a. can be handled by the diocesan bishop as a Pauline Privilege. The marriages described under b. and c. must be sent to the Holy See. In effect, therefore, there are two different types of cases, two types of cases that differ significantly from one another, not just in that one stays home while the other goes to Rome, but also in that the Pauline case is less expensive and less time consuming than the other type of case.[4] In discussing these two types of cases and the differences between them, parish priests and practitioners of the law need a term that is direct, descriptive and juxtapositive. The term

"Petrine Privilege" has fit the bill nicely. It has the right ring to it and makes certain notions immediately clear. "Petrine" shows that, in some ways, it is different from its Pauline cousin. "Privilege" shows that, in other ways, it is like it. It has, in short, proved an extremely useful term and, while not perfect, is simply too good to give up.

B. The Moment Of Dissolution

When Hürth wrote his article in 1956 he saw as a chief difference between the two privileges that in the Pauline it is the second marriage that dissolves the first, whereas in the Petrine, it is the Holy Father who directly dissolves the first marriage "by a positive act of dispensation." This distinction became widely accepted and found its way into much of the literature on the subject. In the *New Catholic Encyclopedia,* for example, the author of the article on "Favor of the Faith Cases" noted that "In cases of Pauline privilege the dissolution takes place at the time when the party who is converted and baptized contracts a second marriage. In cases of privilege of the faith, on the other hand, the marriage bond is dissolved at the moment the pope exercises his apostolic power."

As early as 1959, however, the Hungarian canonist, Joseph Bánk, in his manual on the canon law of marriage, expressed a different opinion. He wrote:

> *When does the Petrine Privilege take effect?* The question arises whether the dispenstion granted by the privilege of the faith dissolves the bond *ipso facto* or whether it merely grants the right to dissolve it when and if the dispensed party enters another marriage. As already noted, in the case of the Pauline Privilege the bond of the natural law is dissolved *at the moment* the new marriage is entered. The same might be said of the privilege of the faith; indeed, the analogy of the two cases suggests this is so (*analogia iuris*).
>
> For in both cases the juridic basis is the same, namely the favor of the faith....
>
> But what is the point of the dispensation except that the parties enter another marriage? And if the baptized parties do not wish to enter another marriage, then the previous bond involves neither a danger to the faith nor any sort of servitude. Therefore, the previous bond is only dissolved by the new marriage of the person for whom the dispenstion was granted.
>
> The dispensation of the Roman Pontiff, therefore, only affords the *right* to dissolve the marriage, in the same way that a negative response to the interpellations does in the case of the Pauline Privilege.

Within a few years of the term's epiphany, therefore, at least one author had already taken the position that the moment of dissolution was a source not of dissimilarity, but rather of similarity between the two privileges. For many years this position of Bánk remained only one opinion and a minority opinion at that, but beginning in 1977 the Congregation for the Doctrine of the Faith began issuing a series of private responses indicating that Bánk's position was the approved one.

In 1977 the Hartford tribunal forwarded to the Congregation a case in which the nonbaptism of the respondent was quite clearly proved but in which the petitioner had no immediate plans or prospects for a second marriage. The Congregation wrote asking for specific information regarding a future marriage of the petitioner. Hartford replied that the petitioner had no specific plans but simply wanted to be free to remarry. Then, on January 17, 1978 under protocol number 1260/77M Archbishop Hamer wrote that the privilege could not be granted at that time. "According to recent grants of the Supreme Pontiff," he wrote, "a dissolution of marriage in favor of the faith is only obtained from contracting a new marriage — *tantum obtineri ex novo matrimonio contrahendo*) regarding the celebration of which marriage the Church should have certain knowledge."[5]

So Bánk's 1959 opinion may now be regarded as the "official" position

C. A Chronology Of The Grants

Prior to the 1917 code, the Petrine Privilege was unnecessary since, in those days, the impediment of disparity of cult bound not just Catholics but other baptized people as well.[6] In practice, therefore, whenever a baptized non-Catholic married a nonbaptized person, the Church considered that marriage null by reason of the undispensed diriment impediment of disparity of cult.

C. 1070 of the 1917 code restricted the impediment of disparity of cult to Catholics alone, and this created a "new" situation. When the marriage between, say, a Protestant and a Jew broke down, and one of those parties then wished to marry a Catholic, would the validity of the first marriage have to be investigated with a view towards declaring it null or could that marriage perhaps be dissolved?

In less than a decade Rome, in effect, answered "in the affirmative to the second part" and the Petrine Privilege was launched. Briefly,[7] the Petrine grants over the years may be summarized as follows:

1924 — Pius XI, only seven years after the code, which recognized no such power, dissolved a marriage between a baptized Protestant and an unbaptized person, with the Protestant becoming a Catholic.

1946 — Pius XII dissolved a marriage between a Catholic and an unbaptized person which had taken place before a priest, with a dispensation from disparity of worship. The nonbaptized person had become a Catholic.

1953 — Pius XII dissolved a marriage between a Catholic and an unbaptized person which had taken place before a priest, with a dispensation from disparity of worship. The Catholic wished to remarry. No conversion was considered necessary.

1960s — John XXIII and Paul VI granted thousands of Petrine Privileges in which no conversion was involved.

1970 — Requests for Petrine Privileges in which no conversion was involved were returned ungranted with a note that a conversion was considered a necessary condition for the Privilege.[8]

1973 — The practice of granting Privileges without conversion was reinstituted by the new Instruction and Norms of December 6, 1973.

D. The Norms

The first norms regarding the procedures to be followed in a Petrine Privilege case were issued by the Holy Office on May 1, 1934, with the notation that they were not to be considered public law but should be observed as internal norms for use in tribunals. They were sent privately to the ordinaries of the world and may still be found in many tribunal libraries. The norms, or articles, were eighteen in number and discussed the roles of the pontiff and of the Holy Office, the conditions required, the types of proof, the role of the defender, and observations about the motives for conversion, causes of marriage failure, religious education of the children, if any, hope of reconciliation, if any, the possibility of scandal, and reasons favoring the granting of the privilege.

On December 6, 1973, the Congregation for the Doctrine of the Faith issued "privately" a new instruction along with new norms. The instruction lists the conditions necessary for the granting of the privilege. The procedural norms, sixteen in number, cover, in general, the same areas as the 1934 norms.

E. General Norm V

General Norm V of the 1973 norms reads as follows:

> Dissolution of a valid, nonscaramental marriage entered into with a dispensation from the impediment of disparity of cult is not granted to a Catholic party who petitions to enter a new marriage with a nonbaptized person who is not a convert.

The norm clearly speaks of a *Catholic* petitioner. Within a year or so of the instruction, the Dubuque Tribunal requested a dissolution of a marriage that had taken place in the Church but in which the petitioner for the dissolution was the *unbaptized* party who now wished to marry another Catholic.

On March 8, 1975 the Congregation replied that the marriage cannot be dissolved. Dubuque pressed the Congregation noting that Norm V did not exclude such a request. On April 12, 1975 the Congregation reiterated its stance saying, in effect, that Norm V should have included the reverse situation as well, namely the situation where the nonbaptized person who is not a convert petitions to enter a new marriage with a Catholic, because, said the Congregation, "in order that a dissolution of the marriage in the instance can be granted, the bond which is established in the second marriage *must be* at least *intrinsically indissoluble.*"[9]

It is, however, clear from other sections of the instruction (see, for example, the introductory paragraphs and I, c) that this intrinsic indissolubility of the second marriage is a condition only when the first marriage is "in the Church," i.e., entered into with a dispensation from the impediment of disparity of cult.

F. The Oriental Law

The marriage law for Eastern Rite Catholics was promulgated on February 22, 1949 by the motu proprio *Crebrae allatae sunt*. C. 60, §1 of that law, which treats of the impediment of disparity of cult, reads as follows:

> A marriage contracted by a nonbaptized person with a baptized person is null.

This is quite different from C. 1070 of the 1917 code and from C. 1086 of the 1983 code, both of which bind only Catholics to the impediment of disparity of cult. This C. 60 of the Oriental Law, on the other hand, binds not only Catholics but Oriental non-Catholics, i.e., Orthodox, as well. Joseph Bánk, indeed, was of the opinion that C. 60 would apply even to Protestants and so he wrote:

> Since the extent of the impediment of disparity of cult is different in the Latin law and the Oriental law, certain difficulties may arise. Take, for example, the following case: Caius, an infidel, contracts marriage in 1950 with Titia, a Lutheran woman. Later they divorce. Caius is not then free to enter a new marriage with a Latin rite Catholic because his marriage to Titia is regarded as *valid*. But he is free to marry a woman of the Oriental rite since his marriage with Titia is regarded as *invalid* by reason of the undispensed impediment of disparity of cult.[10]

Had Bánk's observation been correct then Caius would, of course, be treated quite differently in the different dioceses he might approach. If he approached an Oriental rite diocese his former marriage would simply be declared invalid, whereas if he approached a Latin rite diocese he would have to apply for a Petrine Privilege.

In fact, however, Bánk's observation was not correct since, as we know from a response of the Sacred Congregation for Oriental Churches, dated February 25, 1986 (P.N. 246/63), C. 60 of *Crebrae* does not apply to Protestants. The awkward conflict presented by Bánks is thus avoided.

G. The Petrine Privilege And The Code

When Padre Hürth wrote his 1956 article, he said:

> Having researched, studied and considered the entire matter it seems that those authors are correct who say that the Petrine Privilege . . . *is not included in the Code of Canon Law* . . . and that it is therefore desirable that a canon be added to the Code in which the unique character of this Privilege be described and its use regulated.

Hürth then drafted a model canon in which he actually incorporated the term "Petrine Privilege." When Navarrete wrote his article in 1964, he discussed Hürth's proposed canon and that of another canonist as well, and then went on to propose his own. The stage was then set for the upcoming official revision of the code.

The 1975 schema on the sacraments included a canon (346) on the Petrine Privilege and the 1977 schema on procedural law included four short canons (373-376) outlining the process to be followed in instructing and forwarding a case to Rome. The 1980 *Schema Codicis* substantially retained those canons as follows:

a. The canon regarding the Petrine Privilege itself was numbered 1104 in the schema. It followed the present C. 1150 (which follows the section on the Pauline Privilege) so that, had it been retained in the 1983 code, it would have been C. 1151. It read:

C. 1104 §1. A marriage entered by parties, at least one of whom was unbaptized, can be dissolved by the Roman Pontiff in favor of the faith providing the marriage had not been consummated after both spouses were baptized.

§2. That a marriage dissolution of this kind be validly granted, it is also required that if a new marriage is contracted with an unbaptized person or with a baptized non-Catholic, this person leaves the Catholic party free to profess the Catholic religion and to baptize and educate the children in that religion; which condition ought to be guaranteed in the form of a promise.

b. The procedural canons (numbered 1659-1662 in the 1980 schema) constituted a chapter of their own between the *Super Rato* process and the presumed death process, i.e., between cc. 1706 and 1707 of the present code. They read as follows:

C. 1659 — The Apostolic See alone has cognizance on dissolution of marriage in favor of the faith mentioned in C. 1104 §1.

C. 1660 — The spouse must present to the diocesan bishop the petition by which he asks for dissolution of marriage in favor of the faith mentioned in c. 1651, observing the other prescriptions of this same canon.

C. 1661 — The instruction to prove the existence of the conditions required to concede the dissolution and the other circumstances which can usefully be known is committed to the tribunal or to a priest in accord with C. 1652.

C. 1662 — In the procedure for dissolution of marriage in favor of the faith the prescriptions of cc. 1653-1658 shall be observed making congruous adjustments.

In preparation for the October 1981 plenary session of the Code Commission, Cardinal König proposed that C. 1104 clarify whether the dissolution of the first marriage is effected by the papal rescript itself or by the second marriage. The secretariate felt that section one of the canon made it quite clear that it was the Holy Father who dissolved the marriage and that to be more specific than that was to enter into the area of doctrine. The secretariate, however, did agree to drop the opening phrase of section two, "That a marriage dissolution of this kind be validly granted." This change, it should be noted, seemed to favor the position that it is the rescript that dissolves the marriage (which position König also seemed to favor).[11] At the October 1981 meeting itself the matter did not come up. It was then assumed that the canon, as amended, would be incorporated into the code.

But when the code finally appeared in January of 1983, C. 1104 as well as the four procedural canons were missing.

H. The Letter Of Archbishop Hamer

The absence of the canons from the code created something of a stir. Canonists were wondering whether it meant that Petrine Privileges would no longer be granted, and on August 17, Archbishop Laghi asked for a clarification from the Congregation for the Doctrine of the Faith. On September 6, 1983, Archbishop Hamer replied as follows:

> Your Excellency:
>
> Your Report of August 17th (Prot. N. 644/83/2) asked this Congregation for some clarifications concerning the norms in nullity cases "in favorem fidei."
>
> In this regard, I wish to inform you as follows:
>
> The fact that the canons on the Favor of the Faith, foreseen in the preparatory edition of the Code, are not found in the Revised Code does not mean that the pertinent norms of the Sacred Congregation are to be considered lapsed. They maintain their force entirely.
>
> The competency of this Congregation is sanctioned by the Constitution "Regimini Ecclesiae Universae." On the other hand, not even in the Old Code was there mention of the above norm.
>
> . . .
>
> s/J. Hamer

So for the present it seems we are back to square one. The practice goes on, more or less as it has since 1924, but the code contains no mention of it. Perhaps next time — in the *Codex Recognitus et iterum Recognitus.*

ENDNOTES

1 Urbanus Navarrete, S.J., "De Termino 'Privilegium Petrinum' Non Adhibendo," *Periodica* 53 (1964) 336.

2 Navarrete himself is a dissenter from the term, as the title of his article indicates. For more recent opposition to the term see Henri Grenier, "Can We Still Speak of the Petrine Privilege?" *The Jurist* 39 (1979) 158-162.

3 C. 1141.

4 Most American tribunals request either no fee at all or only a minimal fee for the processing of a Pauline Privilege whereas Rome currently assigns a $200 tax for the Petrine. The Roman process, furthermore, adds an extra six to twelve months to the time required for handling the case locally.

5 For similar replies see *CLD* 8: 1186 and 9: 678-679.

6 Stephanus Sipos, *Enchiridion Iuris Canonici* (Romae: Herder, 1954), p. 473.

7 For a thorough and interesting history of the Pauline and Petrine Privileges, see Noonan, pp. 341-392. See also Francis Donnelly, "The Helena Decision of 1924," *The Jurist* 36 (1976) 442-449.

8 For a copy of several replies, see *CLD* 7: 771-776.

9 *CLD* 8: 841-843.

10 Joseph Bánk, *Connubia Canonica* (Romae: Herder, 1959) p. 558.

11 *Relatio,* p. 265. Two points deserve mention here. First, it is unclear why the question about the moment of dissolution is considered "doctrinal" in regard to the *Petrine* Privilege and so be excluded from the canon, but not so considered in regard to the *Pauline* Privilege and so be included in C. 1143 §1. And secondly, the dropping of the opening phrase of section two by the secretariate seemed to favor a position that was disfavored by the Congregation for the Doctrine of the Faith. Clearly, therefore, even after all these years, the matter remained unsettled.

APPENDIX FIVE

MORAL CERTITUDE

An Allocution of His Holiness Pius XII to the Prelates, Auditors, and other Officials and Ministers of the Sacred Roman Rota, and to its Advocates and Procurators (1 October 1942, AAS 34, 338, *Canon Law Digest*, 3, pp. 605-611).

To see you, beloved sons, assembled in Our presence for the inauguration of the new juridical year of the Sacred Roman Rota, is a refreshment and comfort to Us, not only for what the well ordered speech of your most worthy Dean has reported to Us about your work and the many cases you have disposed of, but still more because this reunion of filial homage was preceded by the devout ritual invocation of the gifts of the Holy Spirit, that Spirit sent by the Father and by Christ to renew the face of the earth. Oh, that under the impulse of that life-giving Spirit, which hovered over the primordial darkness of the abyss, the face of the earth were again today to be renewed! Oh, that the world of men, embroiled by the calamitous clashes between peoples and nations, might blossom forth once more in a springtime of justice and peace! Surely the Spirit of God, who gives Us once more the joy of speaking to you, gives you afresh the life and vigorous strength which you need for the mental labors that await you in the guardianship of right and justice amid the Christian people; whilst Our words confirm, and as it were renew, the dignity and authority which Our Predecessors wished to see attributed and entrusted to the Sacred Roman Rota.

The Spirit of Christ, Redeemer of the human race, who through His Gospel raised to a higher perfection the faith and worship of the true God, also renewed the morals of mankind and of human marriage, restoring marriage to that unity and indissolubility which, as experience shows, constitute the greater part of the matter of your judicial sentences. The conditions requisite for the validity of marriage, the impediments and the effects of the conjugal bond (without prejudice to the competence of the State regarding the merely civil effects) have their guardian and defender in the Church, through the authority which she has received from her divine Founder and which is supremely personified in the Roman Pontiff.

1. In cases which involve psychic or physical incapacity to contract marriage, as well as those which have for their object a declaration of nullity of marriage or, in certain determinate cases, the dissolution of the bond of a marriage validly contracted, We spoke, in Our discourse to you last year, of the need of *moral certainty*. The importance of the subject induces Us to examine this concept more thoroughly; because, according to Canon 1869, 1, in order that the judge may be able to pronounce his decision, there is required moral certainty regarding the facts of the case which is to be decided. Now this certainty, based on the constancy of the laws and practices which govern human life, admits of various degrees.

   There is an absolute certainty, in which all possible doubt as to the truth of the fact and the unreality of the contrary is entirely excluded. Such absolute certainty, however, is not necessary in order to pronounce the judgment. In many cases it is humanly unattainable: to require it would be to demand of the judge and of the parties something which is unreasonable; it would put an intolerable burden on the administration of justice and would very seriously obstruct it.

In contrast to this supreme degree of certitude, common speech often designates as certain a cognition which strictly speaking does not merit to be so called, but should rather be classed as a greater or lesser probability, because it does not exclude all reasonable doubt, but leaves a foundation for the fear of error. This probability, or quasi-certainty, does not afford a sufficient basis for a judicial sentence regarding the objective truth of the fact.

In such a case, that is, when the lack of certainty regarding the fact at issue forbids pronouncing a positive judgment on the merits of the case, the law, and especially the rules of procedure, supply the judge with obligatory norms of action, in which *presumptions of law* and rules regarding *the favor of the law* have a decisive importance. The judge cannot afford to ignore these rules of law and of procedure. Yet it would be an exaggerated and wrong application of these norms, and as it were a false interpretation of the mind of the legislator, were the judge to seek recourse to them, when there is not only a quasi-certainty, but certitude in the proper and true sense. There are no presumptions nor favor of law as against the truth and a sure knowledge thereof.

Between the two extremes of absolute certainty and quasi-certainty or probability, is that *moral certainty* which is usually involved in the cases submitted to your court, and of which We principally wish to speak. It is characterized on the positive side by the exclusion of well-founded or reasonable doubt, and in this respect it is essentially distinguished from the quasi-certainty which has been mentioned; on the negative side, it does admit the absolute possibility of the contrary, and in this it differs from absolute certainty. The certainty of which We are now speaking is necessary and sufficient for the rendering of a judgment, even though in the particular case it would be possible either directly or indirectly to reach absolute certainty. Only thus is it possible to have a regular and orderly administration of justice, going forward without useless delays and without laying excessive burdens on the tribunal as well as on the parties.

2. Sometimes moral certainty is derived only from an aggregate of indications and proofs which, taken singly, do not provide the foundation for true certitude, but which, when taken together, no longer leave room for any reasonable doubt on the part of a man of sound judgment. This is in no sense a passage from probability to certainty through a simple cumulation of probabilities, which would amount to an illegitimate transit from one species to another essentially different one; it is rather to recognize that the simultaneous presence of all these separate indications and proofs can have a sufficient basis only in the existence of a common origin or foundation from which they spring, that is, in objective truth and reality. In this case, therefore, certainty arises from the wise application of a principle which is absolutely secure and universally valid, namely the principle of a sufficient reason. Consequently, if in giving the reasons for this decision, the judge states that the proofs which have been

adduced, considered separately, cannot be judged sufficient, but that, taken together and embraced in a survey of the whole situation, they provide the necessary elements for arriving at a safe definitive judgment, it must be acknowledged that such reasoning is in general sound and legitimate.

3. In any event, this certainty is understood to be objective, that is, based on objective motives; it is not a purely subjective certitude, founded on sentiment or on this or that merely subjective opinion, perhaps even on personal credulity, lack of consideration, or inexperience. This moral certainty with an objective foundation does not exist if there are on the other side, that is, in favor of the reality of the contrary, motives which a sound, serious, and competent judgment pronounces to be at least in some way worthy of attention, and which consequently make it necessary to admit the contrary as not only absolutely possible but also in a certain sense probable.

To make sure of the objective nature of this certainty, procedural law establishes well defined rules of inquiry and proof. Determinate proofs or corroborating evidences are required; others on the other hand are declared to be insufficient; there are special offices and persons charged with the duty of keeping certain rights or facts in mind throughout the trial. What is this but a well balanced juridical formalism, which lays emphasis at one time on the material, at another on the formal side of the process or juridical action?

The conscientious observance of these norms is a matter of duty for the judge; but on the other hand in their application he must remember that they are not ends in themselves, but means to an end, that is, to attain and guarantee a moral certainty with an objective foundation as to the reality of the fact. It should not come about that what the will of the legislator intended as a help and security for discovering the truth, become instead an obstacle to its discovery. If ever the observance of formal rules of law results in injustice or is contrary to equity, there is always a right of recourse to the legislator.

4. Hence you see why, in modern, even ecclesiastical, procedure, the first place is given, not to the principle of juridical formalism, but to the maxim of the free weighing of the evidence. The judge must — without prejudice to the aforesaid procedural rules — decide according to his own knowledge and conscience whether the proofs adduced and the investigations undertaken are or are not adequate, that is, sufficient for the required moral certainty regarding the truth and reality of the matter to be decided.

No doubt there may at times be conflicts between "juridical formalism" and "the free weighing of the evidence," but they will usually be only apparent and hence not difficult to resolve. Now, as the objective truth is one, so too moral certainty objectively determined can be but one. Hence it is not admissible that a judge declare that personally, from the record of the case, he has moral certainty regarding the truth of the fact at issue, while at the same time, in his capacity as judge, he denies the same objective certainty on the basis of procedural law. Such contradictions should rather induce him to undertake a further and more accurate examination of the case. Not infrequently such conflicts are due to the fact that certain aspects of the case, which attain their full importance and value only when viewed as a whole, have not been properly weighed, or that the juridical-formal rules have been incorrectly understood or have been applied in a manner contrary to the mind and purpose of the legislator. In any event, the confidence of the people, which the tribunals should possess, demands that, if it is at all possible, such conflicts between the official opinion of judges and the reasonable public opinion of a well educated people should be avoided and reconciled.

5. But since moral certainty, as We have said, admits of various degrees, what degree can or should the judge demand in order to be able to proceed to judgment? In the first place, he must always make sure that there is in reality an objective moral certainty, that is, that all reasonable doubt of the truth is excluded. Once that is assured, he should as a rule, not require a higher degree of certainty, except where the law prescribes it especially in view of the importance of the case. At times, it is true, even though there be no such express provision of law, it may be prudent for the judge not to be satisfied with a low degree of certitude, in cases of great importance. Yet, if after serious consideration and study, a grade of certitude is attained which corresponds to the requirements of law and the importance of the case, there should not be insistence, to the serious inconvenience of the parties, that new proofs be adduced so as to attain a still higher degree of certitude. To require the highest possible certainty, notwithstanding that a sufficient certainty already exists, is without justification and should be discouraged.

In thus expressing Our mind on so delicate a subject as that of the judge's office, Our purpose has been, in you, to extend Our greetings, Our commendation and Our thanks to the sagacious members of this distinguished College and Tribunal of Christian jurisprudence — in you, who not only understand but are putting in practice the words of the Angelic Doctor: *unusquisque debet niti ad hoc quod de rebus iudicet, secundum quod sunt.* Because the truth is coextensive with being and reality, hence it is that our mind, which acquires a knowledge of things, grasps also their rule and measure according to which they are or are not; so that truth is the law of justice. The world has need of that truth which is justice, and of that justice which is truth; because, as was said already by the great Stagirite Philosospher, justice is, *et in bello et in pace utilis.* May the eternal Sun of Justice enlighten the earth and its rulers; and may He, for the glory of God and of the Church and of the Christian people, accompany you at every step in the quest of that reality and truth which sets the face of justice at rest in the tranquil repose of moral certitude.

Now therefore, with this sacred wish, We invoke upon all and each of you the most luminous favors of the divine Wisdom, as with paternal affection, We impart to you Our Apostolic Blessing.

DOCUMENTS

DOCUMENT ONE

LETTER TO RESPONDENT — C. 1673,3°

> The Tribunal, Archdiocese of Hartford
> 134 Farmington Avenue
> Hartford, CT 06105
> (203) 527-4201

Mr. John Hagdon
118 Florence Foster Road
Chicago, IL 60690

Dear Mr. Hagdon,

Your former wife, Phyllis Crow, a resident of this Archidocese, has approached the tribunal here in Hartford requesting that her marriage to you be declared null.

Our first question, Mr. Hagdon, is whether you would have any objection to Hartford hearing the case. If so, I'm sure the case could be heard in Chicago instead.

I am taking the liberty of sending a copy of this letter to the Chicago tribunal. If you do have some objection to the case being heard in Hartford please contact the Chicago Tribunal within two weeks. It's address and phone number are

> 155 E. Superior Street
> P. O. Box 1979
> Chicago, IL 60690
> (312) 751-8200

If I do not hear from the Chicago tribunal in three weeks I will presume that we have the permission both of yourself and of the priest who directs the Chicago tribunal for us to hear the case in Hartford.

I will then get back to you in the hope that you will be able to offer us your own observations about your marriage, either through a personal interview with a priest in your area or in writing, as you prefer. I will also try to provide you at that time with some information about what the procedure is like.

For the present, however, we just want to make sure that you would have no objection to the case being heard in Hartford.

My very best wishes,

> Sincerely yours,
>
> The Reverend James F. Kinnane

Reference: pages 11-12

DOCUMENT TWO

LETTER TO RESPONDENT'S JUDICIAL VICAR — C. 1673, 4°

The Tribunal, Archdiocese of Hartford
134 Farmington Avenue
Hartford, CT 06105
(203) 527-4201

The Reverend Thomas A. Tivy
P. O. Box 1979
Chicago, IL 60690

Dear Father Tivy,

Doris Passero, a resident of this Archdiocese, has petitioned the tribunal to declare null her marriage to:

> Mr. Michael Crossbill
> 73 Ipswich Lane
> Chicago, IL 60690

Doris offered the names of five witnesses or affiants and all five reside in this Archdiocese.

It seems, therefore, that Hartford is the tribunal "in which de facto most of the proofs are to be collected."

This tribunal would be pleased, therefore, if you would, after discussing the matter with Mr. Crossbill, give the consent required by C. 1673, 4°

My very best wishes.

Sincerely yours in Christ,

The Reverend James F. Kinnane

Reference: page 12

A DECLARATION OF NULLITY IN THE ARCHDIOCESE OF HARTFORD

What is a marriage?

The Catholic Church teaches that marriage is, by God's plan, an enduring and exclusive partnership between a man and a woman for the giving and receiving of love and for the procreation and education of children.

For those who have been baptized, a valid marriage is also a sacrament.

The Catholic Church also teaches that every sacramental marriage that has been consummated is indissoluble. This is in accord with the Gospels, the writings of St. Paul and centuries of Christian tradition.

Although not every marriage is a sacrament, every marriage, or at least every initial marriage, including a marriage between two non-Catholics, is presumed to be valid.

How, then, is a declaration of nullity possible?

In every presumption the opposite may be true. If the evidence shows that a particular marriage is invalid (i.e., that from the beginning it suffered from a radical defect), the original presumption no longer holds. It bears repeating that, in order to render a marriage invalid, the radical defect must be present *from the beginning,* that is, at the time of the wedding ceremony. No defect that might arise *during* the marriage would have the power of turning a valid marriage into an invalid one. When, however, it can be proved that a particular marriage was, in fact, never valid in the first place, then the Church may declare it null.

It is important to understand the meaning of a declaration of nullity. It does not deny that a real relationship existed, nor does it imply that the relationship was entered into with ill will or moral fault. Rather, it is a statement by the Church that the relationship fell short of at least one of the elements considered essential for a binding, lifelong union.

Are there any civil effects to a church declaration of nullity?

There are absolutely no civil effects to a declaration of nullity in the United States. It does not affect in any manner the legitimacy of children, property rights, inheritance rights, names, etc. It is simply a declaration from the Catholic Church that a particular union, presumably begun in good faith and thought by all to be a marriage, was, in fact, an invalid union as the Church defines marriage. There is no attempt in this study or hearing to impute guilt or to punish persons. On the contrary, the purpose of the procedure is to serve one's conscience and spirit.

What is the purpose of the Tribunal?

Church law calls for the existence of a tribunal in every diocese of the world. The Hartford Tribunal, a staff of specially trained and experienced priests, deacons, religious and lay persons, offers assistance to persons who request that the Church study a marriage in order to determine whether or not there is any possibility of a declaration of nullity. The Tribunal then investigates the marriage and on completion of the investigation, declares whether or not nullity has been proved.

How does one request a declaration?

The process is begun by a person completing a marital history form and sending it to the Tribunal. A marital history form is available from a parish priest or from the Tribunal. It asks for information concerning the background of each party and for details about the courtship and married life.

Within a week or so of the marital history being received, it is reviewed by one of the members of the staff. If there is no indication of nullity in the marital history, the Petitioner is so advised. If, on the other hand, the marital history gives some indication that the marriage was possibly null, the receipt of the marital history is acknowledged, a petition is signed, and the former spouse and witnesses are contacted.

What about the former spouse?

Shortly after the petition is accepted, the former spouse, often referred to as the Respondent, is contacted by the Tribunal and invited to complete a marital history and to offer the names of witnesses. This is required by the universal law of the Catholic Church. In some cases, no decision can be given without the Tribunal hearing from the Respondent; in other cases, where there is sufficient evidence to make the facts of the case clear, a decision may be given even though the Respondent has not participated in the process.

It is important, therefore, for the Tribunal to have an accurate, current address of the Respondent. If this is not available, then the Tribunal must have the last known address together with the address of a family member through whom the Respondent may be contacted. Please note that it will not be necessary for the Petitioner to contact the Respondent. The Tribunal will contact the Respondent, and the testimony of the Petitioner and the Respondent will be obtained separately. It has been the experience of the Tribunal that in the majority of cases the Respondent is willing to offer testimony.

What about witnesses?

One of the items to be completed on the marital history is the names of witnesses, people knowledgeable about the husband and wife and how the marriage went. Key witnesses are those who knew both parties prior to and during the marriage. Shortly after the petition is accepted, these witnesses are contacted by mail with the request that they write down what they know about the marriage and send their affidavits to the Tribunal. When the second affidavit is received, the case goes on the waiting list and will be heard in order.

What about confidentiality?

In view of the nature of the information, requests for confidentiality are usually granted. Also for the sake of confidentiality, no information concerning a specific case will be given via telephone.

What about records?

The Petitioner will supply the Tribunal with records of the baptisms of both spouses (or of the Catholic spouse where only one is Catholic) and of the marriage and divorce. Prior to the final decree of civil divorce, no petition for a Church declaration will be considered by the Tribunal.

What happens when the request is activated?

When the Petitioner's turn comes up, the marital history, along with the affidavits from the Respondent and the witnesses, is sent to an Instructor who will contact the Petitioner and Respondent and perhaps the witnesses as well for any further information or clarification that seems needed.

When is the case decided?

After compiling all the information, the Instructor meets with the Judge, the Defender of the Bond and often a psychological expert and presents to them the entire history of the marriage as seen by the parties and witnesses. At that meeting the Defender of the Bond points out the elements of the case that favor the validity of the marriage. Generally a decision is reached by the Judge that same day.

Is the Tribunal's decision final?

No. Church law requires an automatic appeal process.

If the decision is affirmative, that is, that the marriage was, in fact, proved to be null, it must be appealed to the Court of Appeals, Province of Hartford, for a second decision. It cannot be considered final until a second affirmative decision is issued. If there is some objection to the first affirmative decision, the Defender of the Bond or the Respondent may file a personal appeal. This must be done in writing within three weeks of notification of the first decision. When its work is completed, the Court of Appeals notifies the parties of the final decision.

If the first decision is negative, that is, declaring that the marriage was not proved null, either the Petitioner or Respondent may appeal the decision.

Should the Court of Appeals reverse a decision in a given case, the Court of Third Instance would be the Roman Rota.

Is remarriage in the Catholic Church allowed?

If the marriage is declared null and there are no restrictions concerning remarriage, the usual procedure of preparing for marriage in the Catholic Church may be started with the local parish priest.

If a marriage is declared null due to a possibly ongoing cause, a second marriage obviously cannot be permitted until it has been demonstrated that the cause which invalidated the first marriage has been removed.

No new marriage may be scheduled in any Catholic parish until the procedure has been completed.

Is there a fee for Tribunal services?

If, at the conclusion of the entire process, the decision is in favor of nullity, a fee of $300 will be asked of the person who introduced the request for a study. In deference to the people of the Archdiocese of Hartford who subsidize the Tribunal budget, we believe it is fair that those who avail themselves of the services of this office assist in bearing this financial burden. In fact, it costs approximately $600 to cover all the expenses incurred by the Tribunal in each case.

Please note, however, that if for any reason one cannot afford to pay all or part of the fee, a simple explanation to the Tribunal will insure that the case will be processed free of charge. At no time should financial considerations discourage any person exercising the right to receive a just hearing from the Tribunal. One's ability or inability to pay a fee in no way affects the progress or outcome of a request.

The Tribunal
Archdiocese of Hartford
134 Farmington Avenue
Hartford, Connecticut 06105
(203) 527-4201

Reference: page 28

DOCUMENT FOUR

MARITAL HISTORY

Before completing this two-sided form please read the yellow brochure.

(*side one*)

A. DATA SECTION

I.
Self:	Former Spouse
Name _____	Name _____
(Maiden Name) _____	(Maiden Name) _____
Address _____	Address (if unknown, give name and
_____	address of family member) _____
Phone (B) _____ (H) _____	Phone (B) _____ (H) _____
Religion _____	Religion _____
Date & Place of Baptism _____	Date & Place of Baptism _____

II.   Date & Place of Marriage _____

Date of Final Separation _____

Date & Place of Divorce _____

III.   Names and Complete Addresses of Witnesses: (Three or more people who knew you and your former spouse before and during the marriage. Choose witnesses from among friends and family members. Be sure to contact these people and ask if they are willing to answer our inquiries.) _____

IV.   Names and Complete Addresses of Counsellors, if any._____

V.   Present Status:

Have you remarried: _____ Date _____

Religion of your present spouse _____

Status of present spouse at the time of marriage to you:

Single _____ Divorced _____ Widowed _____

If present spouse was previously married and his/her previous spouse is still living, in what Church did the ceremony take place? _____

VI.   Have either you or your former spouse ever applied for a declaration of nullity before? If so, Where: _____ When _____

(*side two*)

B.   NARRATIVE SECTION

On separate pages, prepare a description of your former marriage using the paragraphs below as an outline. Give specific examples of behavior where applicable.

BACKGROUND OF EACH PARTY

I.   *For yourself:* (Please give examples if applicable.) The character of your parents, an assessment of their relationship, who was the dominant one in the home, your relationship with them. The personality of your brothers/sisters and your relationship with them. Your educational background, attitudes toward school, your sense of accomplishment. Social activities and ease in forming friendships. Mental health problems or unusual physical problems. Any behavior problems in school. Unusual fears in childhood or later. History of dating, any other serious romances; if so, why terminated. Attitudes toward sex and related problems. Life goals and personal standards of achievement: religious practice. Number of jobs, reasons for terminating. Problems in adult life, e.g., alcohol, drugs, gambling, handling money, arrests. Evaluation of personal strengths and weaknesses: Ex., Are you sensitive to the needs of others, nervous, quick tempered, moody, jealous, selfish, ungrateful? Would others consider you to be honest and truthful? Would others have reason to consider your conduct erratic or unpredictable, outlandish or fantastic? Would others consider you to have good judgment in everyday situations?

II. *For former spouse:* Please use the same outline as above and write what you can remember about the background of your former spouse.

III. *COURTSHIP*

Length, how you met, source of attraction. Frequency of dates, kinds of things done together. Problems in dating: any serious arguments, breaks in the relationship, how relationship resumed. How subject of marriage arose: circumstances of engagement; part each played in wedding preparations. Families' reaction and involvement in wedding plans. attitude of each party toward children; toward fidelity; toward divorce. Any unusual pressure to marry. Anyone who advised against marrying and reasons for this. Attitude toward and use of sex during courtship. Values most important to each party at time of marriage.

IV. *WEDDING AND HONEYMOON*

Attitude and feelings of each party on day of wedding; before, at Church and at reception. Any unusual incidents? Place and length of honeymoon; was it a pleasant experience for both; when was the marriage consummated?

V. *MARRIED LIFE*

Length of marriage. Attitude of each toward domestic chores and the sharing of responsibilities. Attitude toward and use of sex in entire marriage; sensitivity to each other's needs. Attitude toward children and their care. Physical or emotional mistreatment. Sharing of interests and concerns; use of leisure time; use of money. Part played in marriage by parents of each. When did problems arise and over what issues? Any use of counselors, psychiatrists, or other professional help? If so, please give full names and addresses. Temporary separations, dates, reasons, mode of reconciliation.

VI. *FINAL SEPARATION*

What caused it; any attempts at reconciliation? Please explain. Who sued for divorce? Grounds. who received custody of the children?

It is suggested that you make a copy of your completed Marital History and keep it until you receive notice from the Tribunal that the original has been received.

Reference: page 28

DOCUMENT FIVE

ACKNOWLEDGMENT OF MARITAL HISTORY

The Tribunal, Archdiocese of Hartford
134 Farmington Avenue
Hartford, CT 06105
(203) 527-4201

Mr. Richard Skua
4392 Straight Street
Hartford, CT 06103

Dear Mr. Skua,

I am writing to inform you that a preliminary reading of your marital history indicates that it can be accepted for further processing. Please sign the enclosed petition form and return it immediately.

The people you listed as witnesses and the other party in the marriage case will soon receive a letter from us asking them to write down their observations about your former marriage. Please let your witnesses know immediately that they will hear from us. In speaking with them, however, be sure to avoid anything that can be construed as coaching. Simply ask them to be honest and thorough in their responses and assure them that, if they so request, their statements will be seen only by members of the Tribunal and will be kept confidential. If their written statements are sufficiently clear and complete, it will not be necessary for them to be interviewed.

We wish to emphasize the importance of a *prompt* reply by the witnesses whom you have named in your case. Without the testimony of at least *two* witnesses, we are unable to process your case any further. Therefore, we urge you to keep in touch with these witnesses to make sure that they have responded as soon as possible. Although we have made the initial contact, if it now *your* responsibility to make sure that the witnesses respond. If you find that the witnesses named are unable to provide testimony, please send us the names and addresses of other witnesses.

After the witness statements are received, your case will receive a thorough review and you will be notified of the next step. When your case is ready for further processing, it will be put on a list to await assignment to an Instructor. You will then be contacted for a personal interview before your case is presented to the Tribunal for a decision.

If you have occasion to write to us about your case during this time (6-12 months), please be sure to give us the case name and number as they appear at the top of this letter.

In order to protect confidentiality, no information about your case will be given in phone conversations. All inquiries to the Tribunal must be made in writing.

When a final decision is reached in your case, you will be asked to help meet the expenses involved in the procedure. Each case costs the Tribunal approximately $600; however, we ask you to pay a minimum of $300 to help defray these expenses. Difficulty in meeting these expenses should never be a reason for not continuing to pursue this matter.

We will do all we can to expedite your case, but we ask your patience and understanding since we are dealing with hundreds of cases. Thank you.

Sincerely yours in Christ,

(Mrs.) Carole Bertrand
Secretary, the Tribunal

Reference: page 28

DOCUMENT SIX

LIBELLUS

CASE NAME: _____

I, _____ petition the Matrimonial

Tribunal of the Archdiocese of Hartford to declare null my marriage

to _____ on the grounds of

_____ in accordance with

evidence already in the possession of the Tribunal.

_____
Signature of Petitioner

_____
Date

Reference: pages 28 and 35

135

DOCUMENT SEVEN

CITATION OF RESPONDENT

The Tribunal, Archdiocese of Hartford
134 Farmington Avenue
Hartford, CT 06105
(203) 527-4201

Mrs. James Sandpiper
1404 Crooked Street
New Haven, CT 06511

Dear Mrs. Sandpiper,

I write to inform you that James Sandpiper has contacted our office requesting the Catholic Church to declare null his marriage to you. Enclosed is a brochure which explains the procedure. Please read it carefully and retain it for future reference until all proceedings in this matter, of which you will be kept informed, are completed.

At this time, the Tribunal is especially interested in having your observations concerning this request so that it may obtain a clear picture of your courtship, marriage, and the events leading to the breakup of the marriage. I invite you to provide testimony to the Tribunal in one of the following ways: (1) by written statement, (2) by personal interview, or (3) by an interview conducted over the telephone.

To assist you in the event you wish to provide a written statement, I am enclosing a list of questions which I would ask you to answer as completely as possible. However, if you prefer a personal or phone interview, please indicate your preference on the second enclosure along with the names and addresses of any knowledgeable witnesses whom you would wish us to contact. If I do not hear from you some time within the next month, the Tribunal will presume that you do not wish to participate actively in these proceedings.

Should you have any questions concerning this matter, please feel free to telephone the Tribunal at the above listed number, Monday to Friday (9:00 a.m. - 4:00 p.m.) or write to me at the above listed address.

With the hope that I will hear from you in the near future, I am,

Sincerely yours,

(Mrs.) Carole Bertrand
Secretary, the Tribunal

Two Enclosures

Reference pages: 28 and 39

CASE NAME:

REFERENCE:

On a separate sheet of paper, please answer these questions as clearly and completely as possible. Please note that all information received will be held in strictest confidence.

1. Describe your family background: relationship with parents, brothers and sisters, other relatives; any situations or difficulties which were significant in your own life as you were growing up.

2. When and how did you meet your former spouse? How long did you date before marrying?

3. Were there any significant problems in your relationship before marriage? (Quarrels, family problems, personal difficulties, communication difficulties, etc.) Please explain.

4. (a) Was there any pressure on either of you to marry? Please explain.

    (b) Did anyone advise against the marriage? If so, who and why?

5. Were you ready to marry? Had you planned realistically?

6. When did difficulties begin in the marriage? What were they? How did you and your former spouse attempt to deal with them?

7. In your estimation, what were the main causes of the marriage failure?

8. What caused the final separation?

9. Have you remarried since your divorce? Date of marriage.

10. You may list the names and addresses of two or three people who knew you and your former spouse before and during the marriage. These people will serve as witnesses and will be asked to submit a written statement to the Tribunal. Please advise anyone you list as witness.

Please add any further observations on the marriage which you think are important.

Thank you.

****

PLEASE ATTACH THIS SHEET TO YOUR REPLY

NAME: *CASE:*

I am aware that my former spouse is seeking a declaration of nullity of our marriage. I wish to cooperate in these proceedings.

_____ Please contact me by telephone:

Number _____

Convenient
Time _____

_____ I would like a personal interview.

_____ I do not wish to cooperate.

Signature _____

Date _____

If you wish to be contacted by telephone or to have a personal interview, please note that there may be a delay of several months before you are contacted by an Instructor. However, be assured that the Tribunal appreciates your cooperation and you will be contacted to provide testimony. Please note too that cooperation in these proceedings does not mean that you are in agreement with the process. Thank you.

DOCUMENT EIGHT

LETTER TO AFFIANT

The Tribunal, Archdiocese of Hartford
134 Farmington Avenue
Hartford, CT 06105
(203) 527-4201

Ms. Diane Chat
14 Hilly Street
Meriden, CT 06450

Dear Ms. Chat,

We have been asked to investigate the possible nullity of the marriage of
                            and   and your name
has been given to us as one who would be willing to offer information. Please excuse the
use of a form letter, but because of the number of cases presented, this has become
necessary. A Church declaration of nullity is a spiritual matter with no civil effects
whatsoever.

Many grounds for a declaration of nullity are recognized by the Roman Catholic
Church, and to determine whether or not any are demonstrable, it is important for the
Tribunal to obtain as much information as possible about the backgrounds and
personalities of the two parties involved as well as about the entire relationship from
courtship to final separation. We understand that you may not be knowledgeable about
all of the following points, but any information you can provide will be helpful. Please
send us, in as much detail as possible (typed or handwritten), whatever you know about
the following:

1. *Background and personality of each party* — relationship with parents and others
   in the family, divorces in the family, religious practices, social life, work history,
   military service, trouble with the law or authority, use of drugs or alcohol, attitude
   toward sex, general level of maturity and responsibility, and any particular
   problems of which you might be aware.

2. *Courtship* — when and where they met, length, how they treated each other; your
   feelings about each person at the time; do you feel they were ready for marriage at
   that time and why? Anything unusual about the courtship? Did anyone advise
   against the marriage? If so, who and why?

3. *Marriage* — personality, attitudes and behavior of each; describe them and what
   problems developed; describe your feelings about the role of each in the failure of
   the marriage. Any specific problems in the marriage? Anything unusual about the
   parties or the marriage? Any violence or infidelity? Any marriage counselling? Who
   left and why?

4. *Present status* — tell what has happened to each of these persons since their marriage broke up and give your opinion regarding the present ability of each to sustain the responsibilities of married life. Have alimony, support payments and visitation rights been faithfully kept? Add any other information which you think might be helpful to the Tribunal.

May I ask that you make your testimony as detailed as possible so as to avoid the necessity of a personal interview later on with a Tribunal member. If your testimony is thorough and returned to this office as soon as possible, it will help to diminish the time period for a final decision in this matter. Please, though, do not ask the petitioner to refresh your memory. Your statement should include only your own personal recollections and observations.

At the top of the statement please list the names of the two people whose marriage is being considered, giving the maiden name of the woman. When you have completed this, please sign it and have your statement notarized by a priest or a notary public, whose attestation should indicate that you have signed the statement and have affirmed the truth of your testimony. Would you then kindly return your statement to my attention at the above address.

Last, but not least, if you wish your statement to be kept confidential and to be seen only by members of the Tribunal, please request that explicitly as part of your statement.

My very best wishes,

Sincerely yours,

The Reverend James F. Kinnane

Reference: page 45